"Mike Cosper has his finger on the pulse of the challenges facing the evangelical church. He combines his journalistic curiosity, historical knowledge, and pastoral wisdom in a book that is simultaneously descriptive and redemptive. This is a great read for anyone willing to lean into the past to change the future."

—**Nicole Massie Martin**, chief impact officer, *Christianity Today*

"If I were still a twenty-year-old wannabe Beat poet with a knapsack full of books, *The Church in Dark Times* would be among them, dog-eared with hundreds of underlined paragraphs. Those books were all about freedom, searching for home, forming unique language, and rediscovering an inescapable connection to the Creator and the creation. Now I'm an old musician, and this book will be stacked on a nightstand—one of my go-to wisdom books (like in the old days). I will read from it and pray to receive, as Mike has so beautifully written, a spirit of repentance, patience, and tolerance of mystery. For grandiosity, urgency, and certainty have not served people and planet well."

—**Charlie Peacock**, Grammy Award–winning music producer; host of *Music & Meaning* podcast; author of *Roots & Rhythm* and coauthor of *Why Everything That Doesn't Matter, Matters So Much*

"Mike Cosper has written a parable for our dark times. Through the example of Mars Hill Church under a corrupt and authoritarian pastor, Cosper aims to make manifest the broader corruption in twenty-first-century America that allows a pastor to run a church like a criminal organization—and to have the religiously motivated staff and leadership of the church participate in his narcissistic power grabs. Exploring Arendt's thinking about the power of ideology and the banality of evil, Cosper turns the story of Mars Hill Church into a window to our dark times."

—**Roger Berkowitz**, academic director, Hannah Arendt Center for Politics and Humanities, professor, Bard College

"The church is indeed in dark times. Understanding the factors that have grown this shadow over a long period of time, recognizing that these factors are not new to the church or the human condition, and seeing viable and compelling ways forward will illuminate even this much darkness. This is what Mike Cosper offers in these pages, bringing to bear his extensive work uncovering some of the most troubling moments in the American church, his deep and wide knowledge of art and culture, and, most important, his love of stories, Scripture, and the church."

—**Karen Swallow Prior**, author of *The Evangelical Imagination: How Stories, Images, and Metaphors Created a Culture in Crisis*

"Mike Cosper has stared into the abyss of the darkest horrors of American Christianity. He also has gazed into the light of the gl--- of Christ. This book shows us how to ----- the two while yielding to neither comp------- to *The Rise and Fall of Mars Hill* pod---- shows a way forward without wish-cast---- repentant, cross-shaped hope."

—**Russell Moore**, edi----

T0273509

THE CHURCH IN DARK TIMES

UNDERSTANDING AND RESISTING THE EVIL THAT SEDUCED THE EVANGELICAL MOVEMENT

MIKE COSPER

BrazosPress

a division of Baker Publishing Group
Grand Rapids, Michigan

© 2024 by Mike Cosper

Published by Brazos Press
a division of Baker Publishing Group
Grand Rapids, Michigan
BrazosPress.com

Printed in the United States of America

Library of Congress Cataloging-in-Publication Data
Names: Cosper, Mike, 1980– author.
Title: The church in dark times : understanding and resisting the evil that seduced the evangelical movement / Mike Cosper.
Description: Grand Rapids, Michigan : Brazos Press, a division of Baker Publishing Group, [2024] | Includes bibliographical references.
Identifiers: LCCN 2024019821 | ISBN 9781587435737 (paperback) | ISBN 9781587436031 (casebound) | ISBN 9781493441853 (ebook) | ISBN 9781493441860 (pdf)
Subjects: LCSH: Evangelicalism—United States. | Leadership—Religious aspects—Christianity.
Classification: LCC BR1642.U5 C68 2024 | DDC 280/.0420973—dc23/eng/20240516
LC record available at https://lccn.loc.gov/2024019821

Cover design by Faceout Studio, Spencer Fuller

The author is represented by the literary agency of The Gates Group.

Baker Publishing Group publications use paper produced from sustainable forestry practices and postconsumer waste whenever possible.

24 25 26 27 28 29 30   7 6 5 4 3 2 1

For Paul Petry, Jen Smidt, Tim Smith,
Jesse Bryan, and Luke Skeen,
who, in different ways
and under different circumstances,
each had courage in dark times

CONTENTS

INTRODUCTION

I grew up like the kid in *Poltergeist*, glued to the television and absorbing its messages. Fortunately, the shows and movies I watched didn't steal my soul, but they did profoundly shape my imagination. So when I started thinking about writing this book—an attempt to understand a particular kind of evil within the modern church—I immediately began thinking about examples from movies and television.

An obvious place to begin when thinking about the descent into corruption is *The Godfather*. Michael Corleone begins that story as the son who rejected his family's criminality. But his love for them persists, and when violence is visited on them, he responds with violence of his own. Love, it turns out, is a bridge to an enormous amount of evil. It turned Michael into the very thing he once hated.

That *almost* works. The trouble is this: at Louis Italian-American Restaurant, when Michael goes to the bathroom, finds the gun that's been planted for him, and slides it into his pocket, he knows exactly what he's doing. He's made a choice, crossed a Rubicon into murder. Not all evil works this way, certainly not the kind I hope to address here.

1

My mind next went to Brian Singer's 1995 film, *The Usual Suspects*. Here, we find a US customs agent named Dave Kujan trying to get to the bottom of a bloody series of murders in the Port of Los Angeles. What looks at first to be a heist gone wrong turns out to be the work of a shadowy criminal mastermind named Keyser Soze.

Roger "Verbal" Kint, a low-rent con man and witness to these events, describes Soze as the kind of character crooks warn their kids about. "Rat on your Pop," Kint says, "and Keyser Soze will get you."

Kujan, trying to separate fact from fiction, asks Kint if he believes in Soze. Kint tells him that a friend used to say, "I don't believe in God, but I'm afraid of him."

"Well," Kint says, "I believe in God. And the only thing that scares me is Keyser Soze." Soze keeps others in a grip of fear by remaining a rumor and a myth. "The greatest trick the devil ever pulled," Kint says, "was convincing the world he didn't exist."

The film's portrayal of shadowy evil *almost* works for this book. People do indeed spend a great deal of time arguing whether evil really has a foothold in evangelicalism. This in spite of a solid decade of pastoral scandals, the cover-up of sexual abuse in various denominations, the epidemic of pastoral narcissism, and the ever-growing community of people online who describe themselves as deconstructing or exvangelical.

But where truth parts ways with fiction is in Soze himself. In time, the film answers the question of whether he's real. But what if, when we shine a light into our own shadows, we find something much more impersonal and abstract than one criminal mastermind?

That "something" is manifest in a culture that covers up abuse, enables narcissistic leaders, and punishes whistleblowers and advocates for speaking up. Those who participate in it do so willfully, believing that it's necessary for the sake of the "mission" or in the name of carrying on the "ministry."

Such evil is less like a mask-wearing Scooby Doo villain and more like a fog, hovering in the aisles, pews, and classrooms. The church wasn't tricked into believing the devil didn't exist; it was tricked into thinking that evil was good.

Spotlight and Subversive Evil

There is a film that gets *this* kind of evil—evil that appears good—tragically right. Tom McCarthy's *Spotlight* recounts the true story of the investigative journalists at the *Boston Globe* who exposed the cover-up of sexual abuse in the Boston Catholic archdiocese. The brilliance of the film is in how it resists creating a Keyser Soze—a criminal mastermind who bears responsibility for the crimes they uncover. Instead, it shows how evil can occupy a bureaucracy. When priests were credibly accused of sexual abuse, church authorities would temporarily remove them from ministry, relocating them in short order to other parishes.

This practice wasn't meant to address sexual abuse; it was meant to manage the *discovery* of sexual abuse. The former would require dealing with the predators and pursuing justice. The latter requires "dealing with" victims and those within their circles of influence. Justice never enters the conversation, just damage control. For victims, then, the experience is a dual violation: first by the priest who abuses, second by the institution that pursues a cover-up. The combination is soul destroying.

One scene in *Spotlight* illustrates this point. Sacha Pfeiffer (played by Rachel McAdams) shows up at the door of Ronald Paquin, a retired priest accused of molesting young boys. When she confronts him with specific accusations, Paquin responds with a smiling, confused look. He doesn't deny the acts themselves; he denies criminality. "It wasn't like that," he says. Pfeiffer is baffled, continuing to ask questions as the priest smiles and shakes his head until someone else in the house emerges to hustle him away from the door.

One would expect him to respond with denial. Perhaps, under other circumstances, one credibly accused might also offer justifications—regardless of how flimsy or terrible they might be. Paquin offers neither because he hasn't accepted the premise that his actions require a judgment of guilt or innocence. The categories don't make sense to someone who doesn't consider what they're accused of as a crime.

The evil that is revealed in *Spotlight*—the kind that I hope to address in this book—manifests most clearly in a kind of wound that follows the predatory behavior of the abuser: the response of the institution. Allowance for these crimes was built into the official bureaucracy. Calling it "sanctioned" might be a step too far, but if you followed the logic of the church's policies, the problem wasn't children being abused but the abuse being *discovered*. Such discovery was managed by spiritually abusive manipulation of victims and families, a period of leave for the offending priest, and relocation to another parish. This can hardly be called disciplinary.

So in a sense, when Pfeiffer presents her accusations, Paquin is telling the truth when he responds, "It wasn't like that." The specific words and language she uses to describe his abuses don't register with him because they belong in a different category. Like many abusers, Paquin presents himself as a good narcissist, absent of empathy and unable to think of anything beyond his own narrow interests.

To be fair, there might be any one of a dozen pathologies that could help explain Paquin's lack of empathy: narcissism, antisocial personality disorder, or psychopathy come to mind. But regardless of how severe the warping of his mind and searing of his conscience may be, such an explanation fails to account for how widespread abuse was in the Boston archdiocese and why the accommodating bureaucracy evolved.

As another character in *Spotlight* put it, "It takes a village to abuse a child."

Likewise, it takes a village to enable sexual and spiritual abuse of all kinds in our churches. Our institutional bureaucracies—which might be as small as a steering committee or as large as a Fortune 500 company—provide a structure to constrain the *impact* of abuse while rarely addressing the abuse itself. Each member of the institution plays their part like a worker on an assembly line; none of them realize they're in a factory that produces victims.[1]

The View from Mars Hill

In 2021, I produced and hosted a podcast called *The Rise and Fall of Mars Hill*. Mars Hill Seattle was planted by a handful of people in 1996. By 2013, it had become one of the largest and fastest-growing churches in the country, with anywhere from twelve to fifteen thousand people gathering in more than a dozen locations across five states. Then, on December 31, 2014, the church closed its doors forever.

Mars Hill's pastor, Mark Driscoll, is a charismatic communicator with an eye for the cultural "moment," and he tapped into the malaise of Gen Xers with a message of purpose, certainty, and identity. He surrounded himself with an extraordinary team of musicians, graphic designers, videographers, audio engineers, and entrepreneurs, all of whom saw making Mars Hill successful as a mission from God. When Mark's charisma and sense of authority was combined with their ability to package, brand, and distribute him via emerging streams—social media, YouTube, podcasting—Mars Hill found an international audience.

As Driscoll's celebrity rose, things inside the church grew rotten. Driscoll was temperamental and unpredictable. Staff members and volunteers faced unreasonable demands on their time. Dissenters were cast out and crushed. Policy, official language, and quasi-theological jargon emerged to keep order. A leader would disappear from the community, and the church would be told to avoid them. "They'd gone negative," leaders would say, with little to no more explanation. If you asked questions, you'd be told, "Trust your elders." That was usually all it took. If you pushed too hard, you too might be perceived as "going negative" and, in the language of Stalinist Russia, become a nonperson.

For most Mars Hill members, theologizing conflict and coded language was enough to keep dissent from growing too great. While it was a little more complex for staff and leaders, the church bureaucracy prevented them from bearing too much of the burden of spiritual abuse.

One story mentioned on the podcast illustrates this well. A former Mars Hill communications staffer described how one of his first tasks on the job was to make his way through old sermon transcripts and other written materials to delete the names of several long-standing leaders who had left the community. When he first shared the story with me, he did so off the record, knowing now that these leaders had been unjustly removed from leadership, slandered by church leaders, and shunned by members. It derailed their callings and, in some cases, destroyed their lives.

It makes sense why the staffer didn't question the task at the time. He was new at the job and thought of Mars Hill as a beacon of church done right. Why wouldn't he trust his bosses when they said these folks had done something bad? Within the Mars Hill bureaucracy, others carried out similar tasks. Certain pastors were designated to deal with those who'd been counseled or cared for by these leaders. Others were tasked with confronting the most virulent dissenters. Communications staffers worked to carefully craft emails and blog posts that would get ahead of gossip, suppress dissent, and point forward to the next big thing. A church of thousands of members is going to naturally have conflict, and unless they had a front-row seat, most members were content to do exactly what was asked of them: trust their elders. And why shouldn't they?

Building the Factory

This book is an attempt to understand the internal logic of Mars Hill and other churches and Christian institutions like it where the ends—the growth of the church and expansion of the pastor's influence—justify the means. I want to look beyond the specifics of any individual (or their pathology) to the ideological and spiritual architecture they have in common.

I've spent the past several years examining the current crisis of leadership among evangelicals. *The Rise and Fall of Mars Hill* was the first installment of that work—an attempt to explore in a granular way how people found themselves drawn in and chewed up by a church like Mars Hill and a pastor like Driscoll. My book *Land of My Sojourn* is the second, an attempt at an intimate series of personal and devotional reflections on how an unhealthy church left me searching for a way to rebuild my faith. This book is the third installment. In it, I want to pull the lens back as far as I can to try to answer a question Jen Smidt asked every week in the credits of *The Rise and Fall of Mars Hill*: "Why does this keep happening?"

For one thing, we need to understand what "this" is.

Part of that means understanding the spiritual impact of the collapse of these churches. *The Rise and Fall of Mars Hill* spent a great deal of energy on that topic; this book will explore it more in terms of a social and cultural framework. I want to tell a story here that accounts (in part) for why these stories repeat themselves, church after church, ministry after ministry, throughout the evangelical world.

In part 1 of this book, "Understanding Dark Times," I'll trace some of the history that brought us to this moment and how the church—unbeknownst even to herself—has been primed for this kind of evil by the currents of secularism and disenchantment. I'll talk about how what we see going awry in our churches mirrors other evils in the modern world and how our thinking has parted ways with historic and biblical beliefs about what it means to live faithfully.

In part 2, "Resisting Dark Times," I'll look at practices that are our most powerful resources for resisting this evil: solitude and thinking, storytelling and culture making, and worship. As basic as they may appear on the page, each is profoundly countercultural.

Introducing Our Companion

My companion and conversation partner in this book is a twentieth-century Jewish social theorist named Hannah Arendt. She's been a popular figure in recent years due to her writing about authoritarianism, mobs, and populism—all pertinent subjects given the mood in global politics. But Arendt's insights transcend partisan politics. She seldom serves as a useful prop for any one party for very long.

Arendt was born in Hanover, Germany, in 1906. While her parents weren't very religious, her Jewish identity was never in doubt. She once described being "enlightened" as a small child when kids on the street hurled anti-Semitic remarks at her. She said she'd never heard the word "Jew" before, but it didn't come entirely as a surprise; rather, it confirmed her sense of being an outsider—something she would cling to for the rest of her life.

> Did I have the feeling that I was something special? Yes. . . . Objectively, I am of the opinion that it was related to being Jewish. For example, as a child—a somewhat older child then—I knew that I looked Jewish. I looked different from other children. I was very conscious of that. But not in a way that made me feel inferior, that was just how it was. . . . All Jewish children encountered anti-Semitism. And it poisoned the souls of many children. The difference with us was that my mother was always convinced that you mustn't let it get to you. You have to defend yourself![2]

For Arendt, outsider status—which she would often speak of in terms of being a "pariah"—was a badge of honor, a sign that certified her objectivity and amplified the authority of her cultural analysis. It was a simple fact too. She was Jewish but not religious. She was a Zionist who would never emigrate to Israel and later grew disillusioned with the state of Israel. Though a German, she was forced to flee from the land, language, and culture she loved most because of their anti-Semitism.

America was Arendt's home longer than anywhere else, yet here too she maintained her pariah status. You might argue that she relished it. Many of her fellow immigrants and refugees—especially those wishing to rise in social and academic circles—worked hard to lose or at least moderate their accents. Arendt mastered English (her most important writing was all originally written in English), but she had no interest whatsoever in losing her thick German accent.

A "Tough Old Bird"

I first "met" Arendt in the late 1990s, in an undergraduate philosophy seminar entirely devoted to her work. Like many undergraduate philosophy departments, we were divided into factions—the Marxists, the libertarians, and the rare (sometimes lone) social conservatives. These groups sparred as informal teams in favor of this philosopher or against that one. In the Arendt seminar, though, the factions quickly broke down. In any given discussion, you might find yourself agreeing with her one moment and enraged by her the next.

One day in that seminar had been particularly contentious. Everyone was winded and mentally exhausted. A silence settled in, both because we were talked out and the time was about up. "Well," someone said, "no one won today." We laughed, acknowledging mutual defeat.

Jay Barry, our professor, disagreed. "That's not quite right," he said. We all paused, waiting for him to explain. He waved his battered copy of *Between Past and Future* in front of us. "Arendt won." We laughed again. He looked at the cover of the book with affection and said, "She's a tough old bird."

For Barry, I don't think there's a higher compliment.

Like Barry and many others, I was captivated by that "tough old bird." The image I have of her in my mind is from her appearance on Günter Gaus's television show in 1974. She wore thick-rimmed glasses, smoked like a chimney, and spoke at various turns with seriousness, laughter, charm, and contempt. She writes in a similar manner, often beautifully, sometimes humorously, often impossibly technical and difficult, and always with moral authority. To read her is to experience an extraordinary mind at work. It is no surprise to me that of the people I know who read and appreciate Arendt, most of them develop an almost fanatical devotion to her.

But it's not merely her wit and intelligence that are captivating; it's her vision for the world as a beautiful place, a place worthy of life and struggle. It is the beauty and goodness of the world, of people and places and the great works of culture, that make reckoning with and resisting evil a worthy cause.

Amor Mundi

She summed up her vision in a letter to her friend Karl Jaspers: "I've begun so late, really only in recent years, to truly love the world. . . . Out of gratitude, I want to call my book on political theory 'Amor Mundi.'"[3]

Amor mundi—love of the world—became a common shorthand for Arendt's vision in the years after her death. It's a love rooted in the particularity of the world. *Amor mundi* resists attaching affections to abstractions of any kind, preserving them for what is near, ordinary, and concrete.

This sense of the world as the realm of the particular accounts for why Arendt often baffled her friends and readers. When one of her works created a rift between her and her friend Gershom Scholem, an eminent Jewish religious scholar and Zionist, he accused her of disloyalty to her people. Arendt didn't deny it. She also didn't think she owed the Jews—or anyone else—her loyalty:

> I have never in my life "loved" some nation or collective—not the German, French, or American nation, or the working class, or whatever else there might be in this price range of loyalties. The fact is that I love only my friends and am quite incapable of any other sort of love.[4]

Arendt's refusal to think in terms of a collective hedged against the kind of thinking that had brought so much destruction to her world. Love for a group inclines a person to act in ways that serve the group's ends and purposes. If one isn't careful, concern for the many in the group can quickly overwhelm concern for the few or the individual. To be sure, Arendt wasn't rejecting her Jewish identity, and she maintained a sense of solidarity with the Jewish people. Rather, she was saying that those loyalties and affections—as important as they may be—shouldn't overwhelm a person's capacity to think and judge clearly, including the ability to speak truths that might make one seem disloyal.

Arendt saw firsthand the terrifying possibilities of this kind of groupthink. She saw the land and the people she loved turn against her, not because of anything she had done but because she had become an abstraction to them, a member of an undesirable group that belonged nowhere on earth.

That experience is what makes her such a worthy companion for this book. She spent the rest of her life trying to understand how the most horrendous evil in world history had come to possess the community that she loved. What she discovered was that the currents that gave birth to that evil were alive and well long after the war was over and were shaping much of the modern world.

My goal is to extend her reflections into my own community—one that shocked me in different ways and on a different scale, but one that nonetheless is dealing with a moral reckoning. What do we do when we discover that our institutions conspired to cover up sexual abuse? What do we make of an epidemic of narcissism in our pulpits and the accompanying epidemic of enablers? How do we make sense of ordinary people making moral decisions that are completely out of sync with what they believe or with what they've taught for decades? If we want to see a better and more beautiful church, we must wrestle with these questions.

In the Bible we read, "Resist the devil, and he will flee from you" (James 4:7). The challenge of our moment is in naming this devil, or rather—because it is something so depersonalized and subversive—understanding precisely what the evil is that we're resisting. I believe that's a discovery ready to be made, one that will uncomfortably hold a mirror up to most of us. I also believe that a tough old bird with uncompromising scrutiny and a dazzling mind might help us resist it more effectively.

One of Arendt's most famous ideas is often summed up with the word "natality." We "are not born in order to die," she wrote, "but in order to begin."[5] This is what sets us apart from any other creature—our capacity for newness and imagination. So long as new people are born, and so long as they continue to grow up and participate in the life of the world, there's a reason for hope—even in the darkest of times.

That belief is refreshing in a time when cynicism often rules the day and when bad news about the church seems to just keep coming. There's always reason for hope—from the birth of the

Christ child to the kids who are growing up now and watching the church wrestle through this season. My hope is that with a faithful reckoning, what emerges from these dark times—and what those kids will take possession of some day—will be better and more beautiful.

AUTHOR'S NOTE

Dark Times and Godwin's Law

Before we begin, we have to talk about Godwin's Law.

Mike Godwin was an early adopter of the World Wide Web. In the 1990s he was a chat room frequenter, and then as now, the internet was a place full of arguments, snap reactions, and negativity. He began to notice a pattern. Regardless of the topic, if an argument broke out, it usually wasn't long until someone started making comparisons to Nazis. Most people who've spent any time at all on Twitter (now X), Facebook, Tumblr, or MySpace have seen it for themselves: ignite passion, stir conflict, enter Nazis.

This is Godwin's Law: no matter the topic, any argument extended far enough will eventually devolve into talking about Nazis. Don't want to be a vegan? Nazi. Proselytize your religion? Nazi. Vote for the other guy's political party? Nazi. Laugh at Dave Chappelle? Nazi. Don't laugh at Dave Chappelle? Nazi.

Godwin's Law is in one obvious sense a sign that our public discourse has failed. Rather than arguing against something on its own merits, we shortcut it by likening our opposition to the most brutal and murderous regime in human history. It's a reactive response, a way of swinging the largest and heaviest weapon imaginable in an effort to attack or defend.

It's also grotesque. Given the stakes of most of these arguments in contrast to the actual stakes of the Second World War, most of our arguments seem frivolous or even decadent. Even so, we shouldn't be surprised that Nazis continue to captivate and shock. The horrors they unleashed on the world still eclipse even the most horrific things we've imagined on our television and movie screens. Even when we do find a villain with nihilistic aims—someone like Thanos from the Marvel Cinematic Universe—he appears as something otherworldly, his aims ethereal and symbolic. The annihilation of the Jews wasn't abstract at all. No one snapped their fingers and watched them evaporate. It took place, instead, under industrial conditions, using the lessons of the Industrial Revolution to facilitate mass murder. Read historical documents about the Final Solution, and you'll find the Nazis hard at work to make extermination speedy, cheap, and efficient. Arendt described the concentration camps as "corpse factories."[1] The Holocaust and the Nazi regime is utterly horrifying and captivating because none of it happened *in the abstract*. It was in flesh and blood, concrete and cinder block, mud and soil, gas chambers and mass graves.

So let me say as clearly as I can: the goal of this book is not to make one-to-one comparisons between the crisis in evangelicalism and the rise of the Third Reich. I am not calling anyone a Nazi, nor am I saying that those who have participated in or perpetuated evils among evangelicals are "just like Nazis." They're not.

But there is a reason why our arguments online keep coming back to the Nazis. It has to do with the nature of the dark times in which we live.

Arendt devoted her life to understanding how Nazism took hold in the world she knew and loved. She came to see how totalitarian ideology wasn't relegated to post–World War I

Europe but could take hold in other places and under other conditions. Her work mapped the architecture that undergirded their ideology—a structure of belief that motivated and justified their actions.

That structure has appeared again and again under various political and ideological regimes. In Russia, it emerged with a communist bent. China's and North Korea's versions share some of the underlying principles of Stalinist Russia but with their own cultural inflections and cults of personality. Everywhere, totalitarian ideology justifies purges, exiles, concentration camps, and gulags.

Totalitarian ideology is in many ways an extreme expression of modernity's values—its belief in certainty, in the momentum of history, and in the ability to make sense of the chaos of life. It then stretches these values to a murderous extreme, justifying all manner of evil.

What is critical to understand, and what Arendt recognized as early as anyone, is that totalitarian ideology is profoundly seductive to the modern mind. To minds formed to look for patterns, logic, and consistency, it's like lightning in a bottle. And when it connects at the level of desire, when it provides a sense of purpose and meaning for those struggling to find it, totalitarian ideology becomes an unstoppable force.

The impact of totalitarian ideology on the first half of the twentieth century is obvious. In the years immediately after the Second World War, Arendt immersed herself in understanding how this evil, which had manifest itself in death camps and gulags, had become possible. In later years, her concerns about ideology grew. Rather than learning the lessons of the moral collapse in Germany and Soviet Russia, we had dismissed them or caricatured them, ignoring the preconditions for totalitarianism present in our own world. For Arendt, we were far more readily conditioned for moral collapse than any of us would care to admit.

Not only that, the currents of modernity that readied the world for totalitarianism were reshaping the rest of life: the academy, the marketplace, arts and culture, and spiritual life. The effect was yet to be seen or understood, and to some extent it's still not fully realized. What effect would these currents have on the human experience? On freedom of thought? On the search for meaning and belonging?

When Arendt referred to dark times, she meant that they are dark not only because of totalitarian evil but also because we've lost or been disconnected from a world that previously provided a bedrock sense of goodness and purpose.

My goal here is to ask similar questions of the church—especially of evangelicals. How do the currents that have given us totalitarianism now shape our work and witness? How have they affected the way we think about pastors, leaders, church members, the mission of the church? Have they corrupted our witness for the sake of a political party? Or for an expansionist vision in the guise of evangelism? Have they distorted what we label good and evil, or justice and injustice?

The more I ask these questions and the more I look at the events of the early twentieth century, the more I see Godwin's Law as Godwin's Gravity—that totalitarianism is an inflection point and a moral crisis we keep returning to because, to our shame, we haven't learned its lessons. This too is why Arendt makes a good companion for this journey.

So once again, to be clear: I am not saying everyone I don't like is Hitler. But in dark times, one can fall far short of his monstrous achievements and still land squarely in hell.

PART 1

UNDERSTANDING DARK TIMES

1

Exchanging the Truth for a Lie

Paul Petry wasn't what I expected.

I first met him over the phone in the summer of 2021. I was a few weeks into the release of *The Rise and Fall of Mars Hill* and had given up on the chance to speak with him. I'd produced the podcast based on the testimony of others and the documents Paul and his wife had released online. We were three episodes in, and a couple of episodes away from his story, when a third party called to rake me over the coals for *not* including Paul. I laughed and said, "It's not me—I'd love to speak with him." After several days of tentative texts, we were on the phone.

Given the weight of his story, I expected someone more calloused by the experience. I'd read pages and pages of his emails and letters to Mars Hill from 2007 to 2008, listened to hours of stories about him, and read an untold number of blogs and social media posts involving him. I knew the details of this aspect of the story down to the finest detail, but the moment he got on the phone, I realized I didn't know him at all.

"Hello?" I said when he called.

"Is this Mike Cosper?" he asked. His voice was reedy, thin but not nasal. There was a gravel to it but not an edge. "This is Paul Petry," he said. "How the heck are ya?"

I heard the Chicago accent in the vowels mixing with the compressed syllables of the Pacific Northwest. Like most people, Paul's voice had a fingerprint, and it said a lot about him.

The Petrys joined Mars Hill around 2001, and Paul became an elder in the years that followed. Not long after, he gave up his law practice to come on staff. In 2007, the elders were asked to weigh in on changes to the bylaws that would affect how the church was governed. Paul had concerns. He ran them past another elder, Bent Meyer, and sought advice from another member and the church's lawyer. Petry typed up his thoughts and submitted them to the executive pastor, not imagining there would be any great drama as a result.

A few days later, on Sunday, September 30, 2007, Paul and Bent were summoned to meet with Driscoll right after the evening service. That night, Driscoll had preached from the book of Nehemiah, likening the prophet's conflicts with the elders of Jerusalem to his own conflicts with elders at Mars Hill:

> Now [Nehemiah is] an older guy and he's beating up members of his church. What do we do with that? I'll tell you what I'd like to do with that. I'd like to follow in his example. There's a few guys right now that if I wasn't gonna end up on CNN, I would go Old Testament on them, even in leadership in this church. . . .
>
> Some men need to be confronted. Some men need to be rebuked. Some men need to be dealt with because of that stubborn, obstinate, stiff-necked attitude that "I'm a man and I'm the highest authority and I do whatever I want." And so they need to be dealt with in a very strong manner. He fires some spiritual leaders; certain guys lose jobs. You're not a pastor here anymore. You're out of work.[1]

After the service, Paul and Bent were led to a room where Driscoll and other executive team members were waiting. "Bent Meyer and I were fired on the spot," Paul told me, "right after Mark gave his Nehemiah sermon on beating up his pastors. Little did we realize we were those couple of guys."

That night turned out to be the beginning of the Petrys' nightmares.

Paul received an email the next day, making his termination official. Driscoll, meanwhile, spoke at a conference for pastors and delivered his now-infamous "bodies behind the bus" comments:

> Too many guys waste too much time trying to move stiff-necked, stubborn, obstinate people. I am all about blessed subtraction. There is a pile of dead bodies behind the Mars Hill bus, and by God's grace, it'll be a mountain by the time we're done. You either get on the bus or you get run over by the bus. Those are the options, but the bus ain't gonna stop. We just took certain guys and rearranged the seats on the bus. Yesterday we fired two elders for the first time in the history of Mars Hill. Last night, they're off the bus, under the bus. They were off mission, so now they're unemployed. This will be the defining issue as to whether or not you succeed or fail. I've read enough of the New Testament to know that occasionally Paul put somebody in the woodchipper.[2]

Technically, there was a distinction between being an elder and being a staff member, so two weeks later, twenty-three Mars Hill elders had to review the accusations made by Driscoll and the executive elders to determine whether Petry was disqualified from leadership. They voted unanimously to affirm the accusations. Paul's only path to restoration would have been one of groveling repentance toward Mark and the elders.

Paul refused to accept the lie that his actions warranted the treatment he received. Thus, Mars Hill elders placed him under church discipline—a process that could lead to excommunication. Paul resigned his church membership, and while the elders accepted that resignation, they warned the church community that they could no longer affirm him as a Christian.

Jamie Munson, the executive pastor at the time, gave the church community lengthy instructions on how to treat Paul as an unbeliever, which was essentially an order to shun the Petrys. They lost everything: their friends, their children's friends, their spiritual community, and of course, their source of income. This became a dark and traumatic season of life with spiritual and psychological effects that remain to this day.

Without recounting all the details,[3] I want to note here the subversive evil at the core of how Mars Hill's leaders cooperated in spiritually abusing Paul and Bent.

During my reporting of the story, no one thought that Driscoll's actions and manner were warranted. No one defended the comments made during the Nehemiah sermon or those made the next day about buses and woodchippers. Eighteen of the twenty-three elders who voted to remove Paul from eldership acknowledged as much in a letter to him in 2014:

> We now believe that you were grievously sinned against in that termination. We believe that the termination meeting's content and tone was abrupt, one sided, and threatening. Hearing each of you recount your experiences of this meeting is shocking and sad. By failing to intervene, we enabled a growing trend of misuses and abuses of power and authority that would be feared and tolerated by the rest of the church's eldership.[4]

All of this was apparent at the time. Driscoll's reactive and rash temper and behavior were no secret. But it didn't matter because of the way Mars Hill's leadership followed up on the events. *They changed the subject.*

In emails and public letters between themselves, the offended parties, and the church, the supposedly instigating actions of Paul and Bent got very little mention. Within a few days, the conflict was generalized and, particularly with Paul, made about his attitude toward the church's leaders. He was being *divisive*—a powerful word when leveled by pastors to members—disrespecting his spiritual authorities and "not being on board with the mission and direction of the church."[5]

What *is* mentioned in the emails to the church? Mars Hill's ministry success. In a matter of a few weeks, three separate communications from the elders to the congregation featured the church's growth as part of a preamble to anything about Paul and Bent. It's a subtle but powerful way to say: Look at what God is doing, and look at these men standing in the way. It also reveals the logic governing their actions, which is to say, it tells you what really mattered.

In spite of all this, in spite of the years of grief, Paul hasn't lost his nostalgia for what was *good* at Mars Hill. "When they asked me to come on staff," Paul told me, "I just looked back on my life and I thought, *Wow, everything that's happened to me led up to this point in time, and it just all made sense.* And . . . I think it was some of the best days of my life."

More than Poor Judgment

The Petrys' story is one of a dozen I could outline with similar threads, actions, and consequences. It's hard for many Christians to make sense of stories like these. We have a deeply ingrained desire to give fellow Christians the benefit of the doubt. Even when we concede that mistakes were made, we want to believe they were made in good faith—that a bad outcome was the result of bad judgment, not bad intentions.

But the Petrys' story isn't really about bad judgment. By this time at Mars Hill, Driscoll's temper, harsh language, and impulsive decisions were widely known. And as much as many leaders there liked Driscoll's brash style, few of them would have wholeheartedly endorsed Driscoll's expressions of anger during his sermon or his comments the next day. They also knew Paul and knew that a power play on his part was out of character—or they would have, had they thought much to that end.

In the end, they voted to strip him of his responsibilities as an elder, and they stood by every decision that further exiled, humiliated, and shamed him in the months to come.

The question before those of us who want to understand is Why? If they didn't believe the story as told, if they were aware of Driscoll's faults, and if many of them shared some of Paul's concerns, why would they support the firing?

What do we make of the fact that throughout my reporting, I never heard anyone describe a conspiracy to lie? There were no emails or conversations or phone calls in which someone said, "Hey, we all know what's happening here, but we need to support Driscoll with this vote." In other words, the lie required no prompting, much less coercion. It appeared spontaneously and held with ironclad consistency so long as one remained part of the church.

But something happens when a person leaves the church's ecosystem. Cynically, one could suggest that they simply have no incentive to lie anymore. That may be true in some cases, but on the whole, incentives don't account for the lying in the first place. Nor does simple deception—that they were caught up in the spell of a lying leader and believed every word he said. The reality is more complicated.

Mars Hill created a distorted reality and, within it, a distorted ethical framework. Even among Driscoll's supporters, few would have disputed that he had displayed flawed character and bad judgment in firing Paul or affirmed that Paul's behavior merited firing. And yet, they would have had an ironclad logic of their own for voting to remove Paul from leadership. Likely, they would have reasoned that Paul's actions after the fact justified it by resisting the authority of the elders or that he went too far in criticizing Driscoll. Ultimately, the problem was that by opposing the judgment levied against him, he now threatened the mission of the church. And once that threat was assessed, nothing you could do would hold up under that pressure.

It takes a certain kind of storytelling to make that case, and not just in the moment. In order to access this kind of logic, one has to tell a story about your church or movement again and again, creating a sense of destiny, historical momentum, and the hand of God being with you. That's why the church's communications constantly talked about its growth and expansion, and why Driscoll continuously rehashed his own origin story and that of Mars Hill. It is world building and self-reinforcing, and when you run athwart the leaders of such a community, you run athwart their power as storytellers to frame the conflict.

After the shock of reentry into the "normal" world outside Mars Hill—a world without that self-reinforcing storytelling—the power of the story begins to fade. With it goes the moral logic used to crush someone like Paul. It can be profoundly disorienting, like scales falling from your eyes.

When I noticed that experience among former elders from Mars Hill, it was familiar to me. First, it was familiar personally. As I've talked about in a previous book, my own church experience mirrored the story of Mars Hill, particularly in its spiritually tumultuous arc. When I left my role on staff at Sojourn Church in Louisville, I had to recalibrate my sense of normality. In other words, I understood some of what Paul described. My exit—painful as it was—was far less traumatic than Paul's, but the sudden crash into reality was similarly brutal.

Second, the sense of Mars Hill as a self-contained world, governed by a distorted moral logic, rang another bell. One pastor told me, "You often felt tempted to do the 'right' thing," referring to moments like this when leaders demanded that you support their decision to fire or otherwise punish a "dissenter." "But," he added, "you could talk yourself out of it."

That sense of a distorted moral logic was what turned my attention to Hannah Arendt.

The Origins of Hannah Arendt

Arendt began studying philosophy at the University of Marburg in 1924. At the time, a thirty-five-year-old philosopher named Martin Heidegger was gaining a reputation for his mesmerizing lectures.

Arendt became his student and, for several years, his lover. It should have been a scandal then (as now), since he was married with two sons and she was only seventeen. But the off-and-on relationship, spanning several years before her first marriage to Günther Anders in 1929, stayed a secret until two decades after her death.

In many ways, her relationship with Heidegger is a metaphor for the world she loved at the time. The postwar years in Germany were tumultuous, but she experienced them as cosmopolitan. She could traffic among the elite minds of her day and contribute as an equal—in spite of being both Jewish and a woman. Alongside their romantic relationship, Heidegger was a mentor, directing her studies toward ancient Greek philosophy and early Christian thought. His influence is evident in her dissertation, which focused on Saint Augustine's conception of love. This was an odd choice for her—not only because it was a bit out of fashion to study Augustine as a philosopher but also because it was odd for a Jewish scholar to study Augustine at all in this era.

Heidegger pushed her to focus on the foundations of philosophy, believing it would help her (as it did him) cut through the noise of contemporary thought. For him, this led to clarifying ideas about the nature of being. For Arendt, it would lead her—decades later—to similar clarity about the nature of evil and the nature of thought itself.

Arendt's experience of that inclusive, cosmopolitan world in Germany didn't last long. Anti-Semitism surged with economic and political unrest, and National Socialism began to gather steam. Arendt took note. In 1929, she finished her dissertation and began working on a project centered on the history of anti-Semitism and the role of the pariah in German society. In the years that followed, she watched in horror as the people and institutions she loved came to embrace Nazi ideology—Heidegger chief among them. He officially joined the Nazi Party on May 1 and during his time as rector of the University of Freiburg enthusiastically supported Hitler.[6]

In August 1933, Arendt was working with a friend, a Zionist organizer, to collect examples of anti-Semitic statements from German officials to distribute to foreign press and foreign government officials. Someone at the Prussian State Library reported her activities as suspicious, and the Gestapo arrested Arendt and her mother, Martha.

Martha was released after being questioned, but Arendt was held. Fearing for her fate, her friends collected money and hired a lawyer, but Arendt promptly refused his help, having worked angles of her own inside the prison. "I got out after eight days," she recounted decades later, "because I made friends with the official who arrested me. He was a charming fellow!"[7]

Upon her release, she fled Germany with her mother, settling in France. There, she continued to study and write, working with various organizations to aid other Jewish refugees.

In 1939, as the Germans prepared to occupy the country, she and other resident aliens were arrested by French officials and taken to a women's prison camp in Gurs near the Pyrenees. This was a concentration camp in all but name: overcrowded, infested with disease, lice, and rodents. Prisoners were killed by murderous guards, died from typhus fever and dysentery, or starved to death. Once France was occupied, most camp prisoners were put on trains and sent east where they died in the gas chambers at Auschwitz. Arendt was in Gurs for five weeks and rarely spoke of it afterward—in writing, she mentions it three times, then only briefly.

She escaped Gurs much as she escaped her detention by the Gestapo: on the power of her wits. The opportunity came when the French guards handed its administration over to German and Vichy forces. Amid the administrative disorder, Arendt and a number of other prisoners managed to forge transport documents and secure release. She reunited with her second husband, Heinrich Blücher, and fled to England. She later settled in America, where she would eventually become a citizen.

During these years, Arendt observed countless friends, fellow scholars, and mentors who had been part of an expansive world of ideas embrace or accept the rise of Nazism. She also heard story after story of friends, family members, and respected colleagues who either were murdered by the regime or died trying to escape it.

One can hardly imagine the sense of betrayal and loss that accompanied this moral collapse. Arendt wanted to make sense of it, and she wanted to do so without easy just-so stories. It wasn't enough to point to the mad genius of leaders like Hitler and Stalin, not enough to point only to anti-Semitism or communism as justifications for the death camps and mass killings. She also wanted to resist notions of collective guilt that turned crimes into abstractions. There was a larger story of moral collapse to be told, one that consumed her friends, neighbors, coworkers, fellow students, and teachers.

How had the Western world—a world that for centuries had been on the march to greater and greater refinement in art and thought—given birth to a culture capable of murdering eleven million people? Answering that question would consume the rest of her life.

A New Evil for Dark Times

Arendt's work mapped the origins and contours of "dark times." The phrase attempts to describe the appearance of evil in the modern world, but it also goes beyond that to describe a world where "the past has ceased to throw its light upon the future."[8] The old sources of order and meaning—religious institutions, academies and guilds, monarchies, nations, even the humanities and arts—no longer provide shared values or guardrails.

Hitler's Germany and Stalin's Russia were preceded by three centuries of stunning progress: the scientific revolution, the Industrial Revolution, and the rise of Western democracy. Some saw totalitarian evil as a reversion to some more primitive, pre-enlightened barbarism. The reality was much more disturbing. The evils of Hitler's Germany weren't a reversion; they were the natural progression of some of the Enlightenment's most treasured ideas. This is why Arendt called the concentration camps "corpse factories."[9] In no uncertain terms, she was being direct about the nature of the institution, which was a product of industrial efficiency, mass transportation, and the psychology of crowd management.

The concentration camps exposed our naivete and hubris, and they demonstrated a human capacity for evil that ought to have silenced any proud declarations of "enlightenment." In reality, modernity's progress had cut us off from essential sources of light, meaning, and moral authority, plunging us headfirst into dark times that we have yet to fully account for.

The key to that moral chasm wasn't merely the rise of secularism or the "death of God," though each played a part. It also wasn't primarily due to a political idea like Marxism, Stalinism, or Nazism, though here we are getting closer.

In the end, the key to understanding dark times is *ideology itself*. Ideology first emerged in the nineteenth century as a totalizing way of accounting for history. Only ideology has the gravitational force to distort the moral order of the world so dramatically, as it has proven time and time again since first appearing two centuries ago.

Ideology: The Story of Everything

Arendt describes ideology as an -ism that can "explain everything and every occurrence by deducing it from a single premise."[10] Ideologies "pretend to know the mysteries of the whole historical process,"[11] and they do this by processing every fact and every event through their internal logic.

This isn't the same thing as having a comprehensive or coherent set of beliefs or dogmas. In fact, part of what makes ideology fascinating is its ability to shape-shift and accommodate conflicting ideas and facts on the ground that contradict earlier assertions. An ideology (and moreover its leader) can consume any and all contradictory facts in its iron jaws, twisting them to support the underlying premise.

This works because ideology is structured as a story. Its heart is the -ism itself, the "key" to history that accounts for all that has happened in the past, the struggles of the present, and the promise of a utopian future. In this way, holding to an ideology can feel like having some secret knowledge. Even though the premises of an ideology are always startlingly simple, the ability to reinterpret reality in its terms is a learned skill. It takes time and inventiveness to be "emancipated from the reality that we perceive with our five senses," because ideological thinking "insists on a 'truer' reality concealed behind all perceptible things, dominating them from this place of concealment and requiring a sixth sense that enables us to become aware of [the new reality]."[12] And if that sounds like the way a conspiracy theory works, it's because it is. Conspiracy theories are inherently ideological, offering elegant, simple causal explanations for complex realities.

The Nazis were driven by a racist ideology of Aryan supremacy and anti-Semitism. In their account of history, the German people were destined to expand and fill Europe but had been hindered by a Jewish minority and their enablers. Jews were portrayed as vermin leeching off society and enriching themselves while ordinary citizens struggled to make ends meet. By driving Jews back to the margins, Germans could reclaim the property and wealth Jews had accumulated and pursue a new reich.

It's a simple enough story with the logical engine to accomplish all the horrors of Nazism. It dehumanized Jews, providing a scapegoat on which the entire nation could pour its economic and spiritual resentment like wrath and justify its desire to rob and kill them. It also promised future glory. Thus, those who carried out the dirty work of revolution could take comfort in the knowledge that they were behaving monstrously for the sake of posterity—for a greater, freer, more glorious Germany in the generations to follow.

That future focus is critical for ideology, emphasizing "not what is, but what becomes, what is born and passes away."[13] It has no interest at all in the present, which confronts us, as Arendt puts it, with "the miracle of being."[14]

This lack of interest in the present is, I'm convinced, a feature of ideology that is also a bug. In the modern world, being confronted with the present and the mystery of being is profoundly uncomfortable. By focusing on past and future, it relieves some measure of the anxiety and pressure of the present—which is a key to its seductive power.

An Iron Logic

The power of ideology is its iron logic. Once you accept its premises, it can literally explain anything. When an ideology succeeds, it confirms that the movement is a matter of historical necessity—that it's the destiny of humanity. When it fails, it confirms there are sinister forces working behind the scenes to undermine it, making it all the more urgent for the movement to achieve total victory.

This is also what makes ideology a prison; those iron jaws twist morality into grotesque shapes.

A common misperception is that many Germans "went along" with the Nazi agenda in order to avoid troubles. Had they resisted, failed to report on a neighbor, refused to serve in the military or the SS, they would have been punished even more brutally than the enemies of the state. This is simply untrue. These threats were there, but they largely went untested.

By telling a story that described Jews as vermin who were actively working to subvert the nation's flourishing, the Nazis thoroughly dehumanized them long before the first brick was laid at a death camp. Ideology reframed Germans' spiritual imaginations and consciences, and the desire for a better Germany was a motivating force that turned neighbor against neighbor and made murder a duty of good citizenship. In fact, by the time the ideology had finished its work on a person, the truly evil thing would be to leave the "vermin" alive.

In *The Gulag Archipelago*, Russian dissident Aleksandr Solzhenitsyn contrasts the evil that can be conjured from ideology with the villains of a previous era:

> The imagination and the spiritual strength of Shakespeare's evildoers stopped short at a dozen corpses. Because they had no ideology. Ideology—that is what gives evildoing its long-sought justification and gives the evildoer the necessary steadfastness and determination. That is the social theory which helps to make his acts seem good instead of bad in his own and others' eyes, so that he won't hear reproaches and curses but will

receive praise and honors. Thanks to ideology, the twentieth century was fated to experience evildoing on a scale calculated in the millions.[15]

Ideology can compel that kind of violence because it is totalizing; it remakes people's sense of any cosmic, moral order. Stalinists did that in part by overtly adopting a staunch atheism. It was as if they took Dostoyevsky's warning from a century before as counsel: "Without God, everything is permitted." By eliminating God from their moral order, the Stalinists not only removed the thought of punishment in the afterlife; they also created an ethical vacuum that could be filled in service of the ideology. Whatever advances the cause or mission is good—even if it is vulgar, grotesque, and violent.

Dostoyevsky understood this was possible as well. He depicted it in *The Possessed*, a story about a political revolution in a provincial town.[16] Reflecting on the story, Arendt writes, "If you take away God as the one to whom man owes obedience, he is still left to be a servant. Only, instead of serving God he now serves ideas; he is no longer owned by God, but *possessed* by ideas which act like demons. These ideas are not something you have; the ideas have you."[17]

In other words, modern unbelief hasn't liberated people from their status as servants of an almighty. It has simply emptied the throne. Human nature is such that it will replace God with something that will exert no less authority on the conscience and spiritual imagination. Arendt references Dostoyevsky's idea that man is a "flunkey of his ideas,"[18] and she argues that this is what makes him liable to believe anything, including ideology's totalized view of the world.

Dostoyevsky understood what modernity forgot: human beings were meant to live in submission to something greater than themselves. Or as David Foster Wallace put it, "We're all dying to give ourselves away to something."[19]

Evangelical Ideologies

Ideology tempts evangelicals in precisely the same way that it tempts everyone else: with a hypnotic vision of a rational and inevitable future. It appears as a story about renewal and movement, offering a grandiose promise about "reaching the city" or "reviving the nation" or "changing the world." Within that story is a key to history: if properly addressed, Christians can get in on the momentum of history and experience renewal.

To be sure, I don't believe that most of our churches have intentionally embraced ideological approaches to ministry—the key word being "intentionally." Rather, our world has so oriented itself to ideological thinking that it is present in much of our life, whether we recognize it or not.

At Mars Hill, for example, the ideology lived right on the surface of Driscoll's preaching and was embedded in the stories he told about his own life, the church's history, and his "vision" for the future. The actual doctrine of the church could have been almost anything—and indeed, over time some doctrines subtly changed; only the ideology was carved into stone, and it was focused on masculinity.

One could fill a book with Driscoll's -isms on masculinity. The following are just a few worth mentioning. These are ideas and concepts culled from years of his sermons:

- 99 percent of the world's problems are caused by purposeless young men.
- Reach the men, you'll reach the city.
- Churches stop growing when they stop reaching men.
- The problem with the church is that it's too effeminate.
- The church's biggest obstacles are masculine women and effeminate men.

Together, these notions offer a simple ideological story: The church failed to reach a generation of people because it lost all the men. By tailoring ministry to reach men, you'd reach everyone else. The obstacles that hinder that goal are effeminate men, masculine women, homosexuals, and liberals.

This ideological story isn't about theology; it's about movement—activating people with the same kind of devoted, fanatical energy that we associate with political movements.

At Mars Hill, those who bought into this ideology were ready to sacrifice anything for it, including careers, friends, and family relationships. The promise of the ideology was enough to justify whatever the cost.

Like all ideological stories, once you've accepted the premises, the logic is ironclad. If the church isn't succeeding in its mission, it's because it's being attacked by one of its "enemies"—who need to be rooted out. If someone objects to a decision or direction, clearly they're not "man enough" to lead at Mars Hill.

And once someone is cast as an enemy—for any reason whatsoever—brutal spiritual abuse becomes justified because they're not just opposing a leader or an institution; they're opposing the kingdom of God.

Mystery and Ideology

In the prologue to *The Human Condition*, Arendt describes being at the threshold of a new era in human history. A year before the book was published, Sputnik had successfully orbited the earth. Scientists were describing themselves as at the threshold of a variety of innovations. Soon, they said, we'd be surrounded by unprecedented automation, making human labor obsolete. Human beings would be orbiting the earth. People could artificially extend their lives with computers—what we today would call transhumanism. Or one could engineer a child in a lab, choosing features like parts from a catalog.

Arendt saw these as extensions of the "progress" that marked the years before the Second World War, and we in our relentless march toward them were as blissfully ignorant as those who engineered railways, mass incinerators, and Zyklon B—the gas used to murder millions in Nazi concentration camps.

Perhaps we ought to reconsider our circumstances and progress. In a word, we ought to *think*. In the face of "our newest experiences and our most recent fears," Arendt writes, "thoughtlessness . . . seems to me among the outstanding characteristics of our time." Her proposal was simple: we must "think what we are doing."[20] To do so would challenge us to take nothing for granted in dark times, recognizing that the uncharted technological, cultural, and moral territory is precarious for us and our neighbors.

We evangelicals find ourselves at a similar crossroads today. Our "newest experiences" and "most recent fears" present us with a litany of sexual abuse scandals and cover-ups, denominations in turmoil, weak institutions governed by gerontocracies that protect abusive leaders, and a commercial industry of books, conferences, and other consumer goods that revolve around charismatic pastor celebrities. We need to "think what evangelicals are doing" and consider the degree to which our church's doctrine and dogma have been supplanted, supplemented, or subverted by modern ideology. We need to consider the moral distortions those ideologies have wreaked on our churches and what we owe the "bodies behind the bus" who suffered because we mistook the momentum of an ideology for the kingdom of God.

It starts with asking hard questions about the bold claims of Christian faith. If ideology is best summarized as a key to history that provides an interpretive framework for past and future, doesn't that immediately implicate the gospel itself? Isn't the cross the key to history? Doesn't the Bible make utopian claims about the arc and end of history?

The answer to these questions is yes and no. On one hand, yes, we believe the gospel is the story that makes sense of history and promises a redeemed and restored future in a new heaven and new earth. But on the other hand, no, as the way those claims are presented in the Bible is very different from the claims of ideology. We're not offered a "comprehensible" world in the Scriptures. Rather, we're offered truth in ways that often appear as "through a glass, darkly" (1 Cor. 13:12 KJV), and we're told that faith itself—our inner confidence in the promises of God—is the "substance" and "evidence" (Heb. 11:1 KJV) that what we believe is true.

It's clear throughout the Scriptures that there are things God feels no obligation to explain to us. For example, when Jesus restores Peter at Galilee and predicts that one day, he too will suffer torture and death, Peter asks what will happen to John, and Jesus essentially says, "What's it to you? Maybe I'll just let him live forever. That's not your mystery to solve" (John 21:22).

John has his own encounter with mystery on the isle of Patmos when he has a series of cryptic and apocalyptic visions. The resulting book of Revelation might be the most anti-ideological text in all of the Bible, given its paradoxical promises of martyrdom, suffering, and the restoration of all things. The book was never meant to be parsed like an allegory but read like a fever dream or an epic poem, assuring Christians that their suffering was never happening outside the redemptive and restorative work of God.

The gospel pushes against the rational order of the world. Death shouldn't be the means by which we defeat death. Weakness shouldn't be the way we become strong. Martyrdom shouldn't make a movement flourish, and no one would ever intuitively choose to love their enemies or bless those who persecute them. And yet this is precisely how the church took root in the ancient world and how it continues to flourish in surprising places around the globe today.

When these things happen, it's because something supernatural has broken into the world. Our job isn't to rationalize them or comprehend them. Rather, we're simply meant to behold them with a sense of wonder.

It is a lie to think that we should be able to calculate, rationalize, and account for all that we behold in this life. To resist ideology is to recognize life as a series of encounters with wonders, mysteries, and perplexities and to allow for the reality that we may not in the end make much sense of it all.

Moral Distortion in Evangelicalism

When I reported Paul Petry's story, I was struck by the difference between the letters and emails written to support Driscoll in 2007 and the conversations I had in 2020 and 2021. To be clear, they involved the exact same men; only the circumstances had changed. These men were no longer caught up in the whirlwind of momentum, no longer immersed in Driscoll's storytelling, and no longer watching the unlikely and remarkable phenomenon that was Mars Hill Church. In the silence of that aftermath, every argument and excuse they'd made in 2007 was no longer plausible.

When churches fall apart, when layer after layer of enabling leadership, cover-ups, and moral compromise are exposed, there's a scramble to find someone or something to blame. So we blame celebrity or money, or we blame a naked love of proximity to power. We talk about the idolatry of ministry or cults of personality. We blame theology or toxic masculinity or the absence of theology or the abandonment of manhood. And each of these are, indeed, factors.

But these accounts miss a more fundamental exchange where the substance of our faith and practice has been substituted with stories that are simple, movement-oriented, rigidly logical, and all-encompassing. These stories describe how we're going to change the world. They enable leaders to ask for extraordinary sacrifices from their members in time and money, and at Mars Hill, they enabled twenty-three men to tell themselves a story about how the destruction of one leader was a necessary price to pay on the way to reaching the city of Seattle for Jesus.

Just as Paul describes in Romans 1, we've exchanged the truth for a lie, losing our place as participants in the mystery of God unfolding in time and grasping instead for the iron logic and certainty of ideology. We don't call it ideology, of course. We prefer the more common name: a vision statement or mission.

But regardless of what we call it, we're dazzled by its grandiosity, its promise of movement and energy, and its black-and-white framing of the world around us.

Once we've bought into the elegant and iron logic of an ideology, it's a short path to moral compromise. The urgency of the mission of God has been made indistinguishable from the mission of a local church, and just as authoritarian and totalitarian governments rely on a national emergency to suspend the rule of law and seize power, a similar logic takes place in the church. The importance of "the mission" or "the ministry" eclipses our normal moral reasoning, and somehow what is right and what is wrong are inverted.

> And just as the law in civilized countries assumes that the voice of conscience tells everybody "Thou shalt not kill," even though man's natural desires and inclinations may at times be murderous, so the law of Hitler's land demanded that the voice of conscience tell everybody: "Thou shalt kill," although the organizers of the massacres knew full well that murder is against the normal desires and inclinations of most people. Evil in the Third Reich had lost the quality by which most people recognize it—the quality of temptation.[21]

In the case of Paul Petry and Mars Hill, it was lying that had lost the quality of temptation. That is to say that truth telling and lying had exchanged places. Rather than feeling a conscience obligated to the good but tempted by evil, these pastors—conscientious in every other aspect of their lives—were here burdened by the duty to "do the right thing" and lie.

To show compassion for Paul or his family or to voice concerns about Driscoll's own behavior risked being labeled unmanly, weak, and effeminate. It must have been tempting for some of them to intervene or find a middle way or even stick their own necks out for Paul. As Arendt describes it, this temptation to do the right or moral thing appears in worlds where ethics are so distorted by ideology.

> Many Germans and many Nazis, probably an overwhelming majority of them, must have been tempted not to murder, not to rob, not to let their neighbors go off to their doom (for that the Jews were transported to their doom they knew, of course, even though many of them may not have known the gruesome details), and not to become accomplices in all these crimes by benefiting from them. But, God knows, they had learned how to resist temptation.[22]

When we look at the wreckage of scandal in the evangelical church, it seems we've learned how to do the same. Like most people in the modern world, we've been unable to escape ideology's grand claims to comprehensibility—a subject and origin story to which we turn next.

2

The Birth of Ideology
and the Comprehensible World

I first encountered a church leadership scandal in the early 2000s. I was on staff at a church with a church-planting residency program, and a number of seminary students were preparing to plant churches of their own. One of them was smart, charismatic, and wildly funny. He was also quite a few years older than the rest of us, and his charm and fatherly gravitas gathered followers quickly.

The first sign that something was amiss came during a meeting for community members who might want to join his plant.[1] We sat in an overheated church gym while he gave an animated pitch using a slideshow. Near the end, turning deadly serious, he began talking about the long-range plans for the church.

"My challenge for my members," he said, "is that they'd each commit to leading three people to Jesus every two years. One person every eight months. They'll pray about it, they'll be intentional about inviting them to church and sharing the gospel, and they'll pursue it with all their hearts, and I believe God will answer those prayers."

He eyed the audience. "It's the easiest challenge," he said. "Any Christian can do it. But it's a mustard seed."

He continued, clicking to a slide filled with stick figures. "I also believe God wants us to start this church with sixty members—sixty people who will make that commitment. And if all sixty follow through, look what God can do." He clicked to the next slide; the perspective zoomed out, and each stick figure multiplied into a group of four.

"Sixty becomes 240—just from evangelism, not stealing Christians from other churches. Then, 240 becomes 960." With each slide, the stick figures multiplied, gradually filling the screen. "We'll plant churches when we saturate the neighborhood, and those churches will plant churches." *Click*. Little churches began to appear among the stick figures. "And we'll send out missionaries, all of them committed to making disciples, three at a time. . . ." *Click, Click*. More figures darkening the screen. His voice was rising to a crescendo and the screen was mostly black.

"And if God answers my prayer," he was almost shouting now, "if he keeps me here for the next two decades, what will we see?" Long pause. Then *click*.

ONE MILLION DISCIPLES!

ONE MILLION DISCIPLES! was printed in all caps across the middle of a black screen.

I laughed. Loudly. I didn't mean to, but I genuinely thought he meant it as a laugh line. He wasn't joking.

"Numbers don't lie!" he shouted. "Why wouldn't we have faith for this? Why wouldn't we trust that a simple pledge of sharing the gospel could reach a million people in one man's lifetime? That one man committed to God's vision could see this happen with his own eyes?"

He went on like that for a while.

As people at the church quickly learned, the rhetoric from the vision meeting paled in comparison to the messianic rhetoric woven into his everyday ministry. His reaction to being confronted by two leaders about concerns was nuclear. I came to hear dozens of concerning stories from others.

The slideshow always fascinated me, though, because of the absolute sincerity with which he presented it. It's something I've seen many times since then—a strangely on-the-nose version of the iron logic of ideology dressed up in kingdom clothing. His vision had the urgency of missionary zeal attached to it but none of the ambiguities and uncertainties that accompany life in the real world. Success, and with it the promise of meaning made manifest through a visible church and an attendance roll of a million people, had the quality of inevitability. *"Numbers don't lie!"*

We were the crazy ones for not being able to see that $2 + 2 = 4$ . . . or rather that $60 \times 4^9 > 1,000,000$.

The iron logic of ideology doesn't often present itself as purely as it did then—especially among evangelicals. Usually, it is more subtle, framed as evangelism and church growth. The giveaway, though, is the sense of historical inevitability and methodological certainty—a declaration that says, "If we do these things, we'll see revival."

We call them mission statements.

Don't misunderstand me; I'm not out to condemn mission statements as such. But I am hoping we can examine them and perhaps reconsider some of the presuppositions they carry into our ministries.

Before we can do that, however, we need to understand how ideology itself came into existence, how its absurd grandiosity— the ability of a singular idea to make sense of history's disordered patterns—became believable.

We'll see that, like the rest of the world, Christians crave meaning. As modernity progressed, we found ourselves increasingly cut off from the sources of meaning that had shaped humanity for a millennium. Some of that was necessary. Some of it was a good thing. And some of it was a disaster—and our own fault.

Where the Christian tradition offers wisdom and growth through suffering, uncertainty, and ambiguity, the modern world offered a story about eradicating suffering through "progress," promising an imminent techno-utopia. There was no problem it couldn't attempt to solve, and its record of technological achievement is stunning.

Christianity endured the rise of the modern world, but it was also recast in its image. We'll have much more to say about these things later, but it's worth noting here that modern Christianity is much more pragmatic, doctrinaire, distrustful of spiritual experience, and formulaic in its pursuit of the good life—and its approach to evangelism is thinner and more brittle—than at any other time in history.

These transitions reflect a deeper, structural accommodation of the modern world. Christianity has always been in the business of meaning making and storytelling, but the modern church has shuffled the traditional roles of storyteller and audience. That redefinition made it ripe for ideology.

To trace how that came about, we'll need to wind the clock back about five hundred years.

Rediscovering the World

Hannah Arendt identified three events as the "threshold of the modern age": the discovery of the New World, the Protestant Reformation, and the invention of the telescope. The first and last of these are of particular interest here, since they gave rise to the sense of comprehensibility[2] that births modern ideology.[3]

As early as 500 BC, Pythagoras had argued that the earth was a sphere, and two thousand years later, Columbus set sail on that assumption, believing that the unknown seas to the

West would lead him to Asia. His mission was hardly a failure, though; discovering the New World and expanding the Spanish Empire's wealth and borders made him a hero.

Columbus's discovery shocked Europe, expanding a sense of mystery about what the world might hold. Yet within a generation, the mystery had evaporated. "Precisely when the immensity of the available space on earth was discovered," Arendt writes, "the famous shrinkage of the globe began."[4] It turned out that "nothing can remain immense if it can be measured,"[5] including the size and scale of the earth. By mapping the world's boundaries, we effectively replaced the question marks at the borders of our imagination with a period.

What happened with the mapping of the New World would occur again and again in the modern age. Each discovery eroded mystery. With mystery comes an infinite sense of possibility: Could heaven lie at the other side of the sea? Could hell? Could it be populated with angels or monsters? An advanced civilization? Untold riches?

But no matter what the explorers found, the results were the same. Certainty replaced mystery, the infinite became finite, and the world became locked within the closed walls of comprehensibility.

Nearly 450 years would separate the Ferdinand Magellan expedition's journey around the world and the first photos of earth from space, and yet both redefined the earth's limits and rapidly transformed how men and women conceptualized it.

As such, the world shrank down into something we can spin in our hands, giving rise to comprehensibility. It also gave us a universalized perspective—a sense that in order to comprehend our world, our cosmos, and ourselves, we have to remove ourselves from it. Arendt writes:

> It is in the nature of the human surveying capacity that it can function only if man disentangles himself from all involvement

in and concern with the close at hand and withdraws himself to a distance from everything near him.[6]

We do something similar in ordinary life when we step back after hanging a picture or painting a room, for example. Marriages often require an objective perspective from a counselor. Human resources directors are meant to serve this role as objective outsiders in workplace conflicts.

Arendt argues something further though. We make the objective move—meaning, we virtually or conceptually remove ourselves as residents of the earth to take on a universal perspective. The world is now a subject we consider in the abstract, as though we were looking at it "from the viewpoint of the universe,"[7] not as the place we are a part of.

The world, reconceived in this way, is *not* naturally or immediately conceived as the ground beneath our feet, the air we breathe, and the place we lay our head at night. Instead, it's an *object* of study and theory, something external to us. As such, Arendt argues, the way we think about our actions upon it are conceived in ways that once would have been unimaginable.

This is starkly illustrated in a scene from Christopher Nolan's movie *Oppenheimer*. On the night before the test of the first atomic bomb, General Groves (played by Matt Damon) overhears some of the physicists who worked on the project joking that the bomb could cause a chain reaction and incinerate the earth's atmosphere. Moments before the test, he asks J. Robert Oppenheimer (played by Cillian Murphy) about it, who assures him that while those calculations did trouble them at one point, they'd looked at it and didn't think it was a significant possibility. Groves is incredulous.

"Are you saying there's a chance that when we push that button, we destroy the world?"

"The chances are near zero," Oppenheimer says.

Groves repeats him. "*Near* zero?"

"What do you want from theory alone?" Oppenheimer asks. "Zero would be nice."[8]

Nolan's portrayal of Oppenheimer is someone with a mind obsessed with possibility and numb to consequences.

These transgressions come back to haunt him late in life, just as the shock of the bomb and the brutality of its consequences shock him. No one can say, "We couldn't have imagined the consequences," because, of course, they could and did and dropped the bomb anyway. Nolan's portrayal brilliantly highlights the inescapability of consequences. Oppenheimer's calculations might have been an abstraction, but the consequences were real-world and dreadful.

Perhaps never was the myth of objectivity so necessary, and its consequences so deadly, as in the Manhattan Project. Its participants believed they were dealing in abstractions, and that gave them the distance needed to build and test a weapon that could destroy the world and all of life.

To be sure, seeking objectivity isn't inherently evil. But when we do seek it, we might be inviting downstream consequences. Much of the history of the modern age—with its disastrous wars and its ravaging impact on the environment—came about because men and women believed they'd achieved this objective and wider perspective. Our failures testify to the limits of our foresight.

To put it another way: before we could indulge delusions of grandeur about a church that was going to "change the world," we had to adopt a point of view that believed the world could be perceived in its entirety. That sense of distance and remove is a prerequisite to the logic that allows for that sort of grandiosity (and the abuse that often accompanies it).

Discovering the Universe

Arendt also identifies the telescope as helping to mark the dawn of the modern age. Originally designed to be a tool for the military—an enormous spyglass—the telescope soon made its way throughout Europe, capturing the attention of an Italian polymath named Galileo Galilei in 1609. Soon enough, he built his own: it was twenty meters long, made of wood and glass, and magnified an image twenty times greater than the capacity of the human eye.

On January 7, 1610, Galileo pointed his telescope at Jupiter for the first time, noticing three stars suspended very close to the giant planet. Over the next few nights, he observed these stars as they moved in nonsensical ways across the sky. Sometimes they seemed to disappear behind Jupiter, or they obscured one another.

By January 15, he'd identified four objects and determined that they were in fact not stars but moons orbiting Jupiter. The implications were enormous. Galileo had documented the existence of celestial objects that did not orbit the earth, meaning the earth was not in fact at the center of the universe. This refuted church dogma that placed the earth firmly and immovably at the center of the universe (more on this in chap. 4). Two months later, he published his findings in a booklet titled *The Starry Messenger*, and the scientific revolution was born.

Sixty years before Galileo, Nicholas Copernicus had observed the movement of the planets (without the aid of a telescope) and noticed that their paths were elliptical and occasionally retrograde—appearing to move backward. Copernicus theorized that the earth was rotating around the sun, and offered proof in the form of mathematics. His theories roused the church's suspicion, but their response was hardly scandalous since it was primarily argued with math—a realm of abstraction and theory.

Galileo's achievement bridged those abstractions, making Copernicus's math undeniable. With clever geometry, he could extend his discoveries even beyond what was perceptible with the telescope, revealing the height of the mountains on the moon.

Imagine the dizzying effect of it. Galileo makes no claims of magical or supernatural power. Instead, he simply observes what anyone else could have if they'd had the skill to build a telescope and the foresight to look. His revelations gave us insight and answers to questions we didn't know we had.

With the telescope, Arendt writes (quoting Galileo), "the secrets of the universe were delivered to human cognition 'with the certainty of sense perception.'"[9] Here we find a parallel irony to that of the success of the explorers. Galileo proved humanity could expose the universe's secrets via scientific inquiry and technology. And yet, this achievement simultaneously shattered human confidence in our senses as the bedrock of knowledge. It turned out that sunrises and sunsets and the earth's fixed place were illusions. Moreover, we were the subjects of complicated clockworks we could not directly see, feel, or comprehend— that is, until we described it in the symbolic language of math and documented it with tools of our own design.

The irony, again, is that while the triumph of the sciences opened vistas of knowledge, making these "secrets" known, it did so by constructing a new enclosure of logic, mathematics, and abstraction. As Arendt puts it, "Modern men were not thrown back upon this world but upon themselves,"[10] away from sense experience and into the world inside our heads.

As a result, we moderns are intuitively skeptical about our actual, everyday experiences. To put it in terms that will be familiar to those who have sought to understand spiritually abusive communities: we are primed for the experience of gaslighting—when someone tells us not to believe our own lying eyes. We're used to encountering things in the world and believing that we require a complex, rational story to make sense of them.

The inverse is also true: we're suspicious of what our senses tell us but wildly confident that math or logic can account for the phenomena we encounter. The implications of this are profound.

Within a generation of Galileo's revelations, René Descartes introduced the concept of radical doubt, subjecting all belief and perception to the rigors of logic and reducing what could be known with any certainty to the thinking self. His familiar "I think therefore I am" flows naturally from a loss of confidence in the senses that followed Galileo, giving birth to an era of philosophy that Paul Ricoeur famously called the "school of suspicion."[11]

As Arendt describes it:

> Despair and triumph are inherent in the same event. If we wish to put this into historical perspective, it is as if Galileo's discovery proved in demonstrable fact that both the worst fear and the most presumptuous hope of human speculation . . . could only come true together.[12]

In other words, we lost touch with the real world at the precise moment we mastered it. We mastered it through technology, reason, and abstraction. We lost it because these tools revealed that we could not trust how it presented itself to us directly, through our senses.

History and Ideology

Descartes took enough pride in his revolutionary approach that he declared himself the first philosopher to succeed in philosophy.[13] One can almost understand it (if not forgive it) because this too was a foretaste of something to come. Grandiosity would be a hallmark of the era to follow him. There were no more mysteries left in the natural world, just problems to solve with logic and mathematics. Solve the math, and anything was possible.

Five hundred years later, that grandiosity is all the more deeply rooted in our imaginations. There is nothing we cannot achieve, so long as we're able to find the right formula—chemical or mathematical. In the church, there's nothing we can't achieve for God; the right strategy will yield extraordinary kingdom results.

Or one church, with the faith of a mustard seed, can grow predictably and exponentially, all the way to one million disciples. Remember: the numbers don't lie.

As the Enlightenment unfolded, the sense emerged that social and political life would yield itself to the scientific method as well. If we could make sense of weather and dysentery, why not economic inequality and the dignity of man?

Alexis de Tocqueville demonstrated this optimism in his introduction to *Democracy in America*. He began by describing how achievements in the marketplace, sciences, and academy contributed to the success of democracy.

For Tocqueville, then, the next step would require applying Enlightenment wisdom and methods to human affairs. "A new political science is needed for a world altogether new," he wrote.[14]

It was a common sentiment. Why couldn't we use our faculties of reason and our capacity to organize ideas in a way that not only made sense of our social and political history but also helped us to usher in a present that is ruled by reason?

This was the impulse behind the work of Georg Friedrich Wilhelm Hegel, and it gave birth to the social sciences and a new area of inquiry for philosophers: the philosophy of history.

Hegel reintroduced history as a single, comprehensible story. Its events could be discerned as a rational dialogue of thesis, antithesis, and synthesis. The French Revolution was one of the most obvious examples to Hegel, where the aristocracy made one claim to rule (thesis), the revolutionaries another (antithesis), and the French Republic emerged from the conflict (synthesis—better than the two).

Hegel believed that innumerable "dialogues" like this one would take place during the march of history, resulting ultimately in a more just, virtuous world.

This was the final ingredient in the birth of ideology, though Hegel hadn't quite achieved it yet. His work still focused on abstractions—thesis, antithesis, synthesis—which left a person without clarity or certainty about where, in the moment, they stood in the chain of historical development. The template was there, but someone needed to make it concrete.

Enter Karl Marx.

Seeing the Future

Marx liked Hegel's thesis about the historical process, but he injected an even bolder idea: if the philosopher were able to discern the historical process, why wouldn't they accelerate it—even by force?

Marx was a materialist and had no interest in ancient philosophical categories of transcendence or in Hegel's "absolute spirit." The actual material conditions and experiences of men and women—specifically their economic conditions—should be the first order of concern. This would make the affairs of men—history and politics—the primary subjects of philosophy and, properly understood, could lead to greater material flourishing.

Marx zeroed in on class struggle, and communism was born. In one sense, this is simply an extension of the idea of comprehensibility birthed three centuries earlier with the circumnavigation of the globe and the invention of the telescope. Only, rather than relying on the discernible logic of physics that governs the universe's building blocks, it looks for key human factors, conflicts, or desires, counting on a universality similar to gravity. Countless others—historians, philosophers, politicians, and revolutionaries—followed in Marx's footsteps, searching history for a key that would unlock its logic and make sense of both past and future. Arendt writes:

> Marx was only the first—and still the greatest, among historians—to mistake a pattern for a meaning, and he certainly could hardly have been expected to realize that there was almost no pattern into which the events of the past would not have fitted as neatly and consistently as they did into his own.[15]

His real contribution, in other words, wasn't centering class struggle as the key to history; it was the notion of a key to history—the idea that one could identify a force or a conflict that accounted for the problems and process of history.

> Marx's pattern at least was based on one important historical insight; since then we have seen historians freely imposing upon the maze of past facts almost any pattern they wish, with the result that the ruin of the factual and particular through the seemingly higher validity of general "meanings" has even undermined the basic factual structure of all historical process, that is, chronology.[16]

In Arendt's view, this defined the modern age more than any other ideal.

> To our modern way of thinking nothing is meaningful in and by itself, not even history or nature taken each as a whole, and certainly not particular occurrences in the physical order or specific historical events. . . . The process, which alone makes meaningful whatever it happens to carry along, has thus acquired a monopoly on meaning and significance.[17]

To put it another way, we're all Marxists now, not because we share utopian ideals and certainly not because we're all communists, but because his underlying idea—that history is a comprehensible, logical, and linear process—has won the day so completely that it's hardly called into question.

This is the foundational template for ideology, the one in whose image every -ism or theory of history has been made. Class struggle can easily be substituted with other keys that explain the events of the past and point a way to a utopian future, whether that's a concept of racial superiority, free markets, other forms of socialism, religious authority, or—in examples that are less effective but nonetheless real—health and wellness, animal rights, or sexual liberation. The list is endless and stretches far beyond the realm of politics and economics. Ideology is what appears whenever someone claims to have a simple, all-explaining idea that can change the world. In our churches, this is often referred to as a mission statement.

Institutions versus Movements

Our modern ideology of progress is evident in broadly shared assumptions—for instance, the oft-memed phrase, "The future is here; where's my flying car?" or the casual way we assume that any given problem—from cancer to climate change—will find a technological solution. Our default setting is to believe that the problem can be solved; it is actually more difficult to imagine what we might do as a society if they go unsolved.

American politics remains a place where the notion of progress is contested. For the better part of sixty years, Americans have debated the role and effectiveness of governmental interventions in social life, culture, and education. The political left has leaned into the idea of progress at many levels, envisioning a society made better through technocratic oversight and social engineering.

William F. Buckley defined a conservative as one who stood athwart history crying, "Stop!" From the time he published *God and Man at Yale*, he was the intellectual head of a movement that distrusted progress and doubted the state could manage the task of social and economic engineering. It's a defensible position when one is talking about trade rules and taxes or in the creep of secularism or socialist economic dogma. It's less defensible when it becomes a bulwark against the civil rights of women and minorities. One can easily see how crying "stop" during the "I Have a Dream" speech or the Montgomery bus boycotts is not only a bad look but bad ethics.

This helpfully distinguishes between a principle and an ideology—distrust of progress or social engineering can be a good thing, but if it becomes an iron law, a necessary interpretive logic for every historical event, it births moral monstrosities.

Buckley had a massive influence on the right, but it would be inaccurate to say that the right in America is consistently conservative—especially in our given moment. Often, with surging populist sentiment, the right shows itself just as willing to indulge an ideology of progress that looks to technocratic solutions to accomplish its ends, whether that's in terms of protectionist trade policy, book banning, or legislating against Drag Queen Story Hour. The right's ideology of progress is identical to the left's; it's rooted in the belief that human ingenuity and well-ordered policy can produce a more moral society than one rooted in libertarian freedom. Only its premises are different.

One feature of ideology that is most obvious in the progressive left is its ever-expansive reach. For example, progressive principles do deserve credit for important victories against injustice, including elements of the civil rights movement and women's suffrage. (These were also supported by Christian principles of human dignity.) In the beginning, they were directed toward equal protection of all people under the law. However, over time elements of their movement (and many who came in its footsteps) supplanted their founding principles with an ideology of progress. This meant that progress itself became the reason for the movement, not the principles or specific outcomes. With each victory, new frontiers of oppression need to be identified to continue the energy and momentum of the movement.

Thus, organizations like the Southern Poverty Law Center or the Rainbow Push Coalition became advocates for gender ideology, medical interventions for gender dysphoria, and gay marriage. It doesn't matter that these issues do not follow logically from the premises of their origins or that they oppose many of the sources of moral authority that were the foundation of that movement. The same can be said of the American Civil Liberties Union, which was founded on principles of free speech absolutism but—because of ideological commitments that are in conflict with those principles—now works to limit speech that it sees as violent or dangerous.

The rise of Donald Trump must be understood in part as the triumph of an ideology of grievance, with him standing in (as he said in the speech announcing the launch of his 2024 presidential race) as the people's "retribution." It's as if his template for the speech came from *Veep*'s Jonah Ryan who during his campaign announcement said:

> Let's send [Washington insiders] a message, by shoving the guy that they hate the most right back in their faces. Today, I am announcing my exploratory committee for the President of the United States, which means that I am basically definitely running.[18]

The Atlantic's Adam Serwer famously said of Trump and his allies, "The cruelty is the point," which I think is partially right except that it misses the extent to which the cruelty is meant for display, not simply to inflict harm on others. In other words, the *provocation* is the point; it feeds the mob's need for evidence that Trump is indeed fighting and inflicting harm on "them"—the abstract villain in his story.

Each of these examples demonstrates how ideology co-opts institutions, transforming them into ideological movements. The turns are often subtle, indicated more by action than language, since many of these institutions would still claim the principles and language that defined their origins. In this way, they're useful as analogs to help us understand what happened in the church.

Evangelicals, World Changing, and Ideology

It can sometimes be difficult to distinguish between ideology and Christian doctrine. One might reasonably ask, "What's wrong with utopianism?" since Christianity makes grandiose promises about the future, or "What's wrong with certainty?" since Christianity demands faith. The answer to each of these questions is, "Maybe nothing."

The better question to ask in order to distinguish between principled beliefs and ideological beliefs is, "What do we possess?"

On the question of faith and certainty, we might consider how Christianity became comprehensible through seamless dogma. The same thing holds true with final things (utopia); we might consider how we became so certain about what Scripture tells us we can only see "through a glass, darkly." Most importantly, we ought to observe our hearts and attitudes toward those who don't hold their convictions quite like we do.

But what we see often in the modern world is movements within Christianity where one doctrine—be it gender and masculinity, seven-day creation, or a specific theory of the end times (to name just a few)—becomes the litmus test for true faith and the key belief for interpreting all others. Such a commitment often orients the life and practices of the church in ways that are distorting—and it justifies doing so with rigorous logic.

We also know ideology is afoot in the church when we lose sight of the distinction between the local church and the church universal. This actually came up during *The Rise and Fall of Mars Hill* and resulted in quite a bit of negative feedback. It wasn't about Mark Driscoll, though; it was about Bill Hybels, the founder of Willow Creek Community Church in the Chicago suburbs.

Hybels was probably the single most influential pastor of the 1990s and early 2000s, a megachurch pioneer celebrated by politicians, CEOs, and world leaders. In 2018, allegations emerged about inappropriate sexual behavior by Hybels, including sexual harassment and sexual assault.

On the podcast, I included an audio clip of Hybels speaking at a Global Leadership Summit, an annual event he hosted for pastors and leaders around the world. In that clip, he said, "Willow [Creek] has to reach its potential because [dramatic pause] it's the hope of the world."[19]

The church is the hope of the world to the extent that it is responsible for bearing witness to the good news to the world. But not *this* church or *that* church; rather, the universal church, which is made up of all who are washed in the blood of the Lamb. Our individual churches are, at best, brief, visible expressions of that larger community and larger hope. The grass withers and flowers fade, and our local institutions—important as they may be—are hardly more resilient than these. But God's Word and his church advance just fine whether your church, my church, or Willow Creek "reaches its potential" or not. Sometimes the church might advance when a particular local church implodes.

Some listeners thought I had taken Hybels's words out of context. They argued that he was talking about the church *in general* being the hope of the world. I was well aware of the context, of course, and I don't think I misrepresented it. Blurring the distinction between local and universal was the point of the talk, heightening the sense of urgency around the success of *this particular church* as well as its pastors. Hybels's statement reveals an ideology in which his local church was the center of an ideological movement, and he was advocating for other leaders to do the same.

Even the language of "reaching its potential" is fascinating. Who's to say what Willow Creek's potential was? The obvious answer is "God," but Hybels wasn't leaving it in God's hands to wait and see; he was making a claim of comprehensibility. The mission of God can be understood, engineered, and manifested by direct action through a well-cast vision and a well-executed strategic plan.

In other words, the key to advancing the gospel is good management. Strong executive leaders, innovation, and entrepreneurship would turn a mustard seed into the mightiest tree in the forest. Conversely, the great obstacles for the mission—the reasons it *wasn't* succeeding apart from leaders like Hybels—were weak leaders, uninspired and unimaginative leaders, and a people with no vision.

Thus, an iron logic is formed that empowers a leader like Hybels to control the organization. With success, that logic only becomes stronger, expanding to justify the tolerance or cover-up of the kind of disqualifying behavior Hybels is accused of. The mission, we are told, is too urgent to disrupt it for the sake of accountability.

Ideology is seductive precisely because it offers us a vision of spiritual and ecclesial life unbound by the experiences of failure, spiritual forgetfulness, and suffering. "Success" is comprehensible and achievable—just so long as we remain ruthlessly committed to the core idea, the theory of everything. We can reach our city, change the world, or even make one million disciples because the numbers (and the iron logic) never lie.

Meanwhile, the decline of a local church is part of the redemptive story of the New Testament. We read of Paul planting the church at Ephesus in Acts 19 and 20. When he writes his epistle to them later, they're being tested by false teachers, moral decline, division, and persecution. Then, in Revelation 2, they're commended for testing the truth and rejecting false apostles, but they're also warned that God is about to remove their lampstand—their sense of his blessing and presence—because they've lost their first love.

In many ways, it's a bleak story. They seemed to get what Paul told them, but they lost something more essential in the process. And yet, the book of Revelation tells a much larger story in which ambiguity about the church at Ephesus's future is ultimately overshadowed by the defeat of the devil and the victory of the kingdom of God. It's a clear, sobering message that our communities may not last forever, and that redemption doesn't depend on them.

One could imagine an honest church mission statement based on these warnings: "So-and-So Community Church. Here in fear and trembling until God removes our lampstand." Most consultants would counsel against it (though with the right marketing campaign, it might be quite effective among a certain stripe of tired evangelicals), but it would be far more honest than the vision statements that promise to reach the four corners of the earth, serve the entire city, or change the world.

Regardless of what reform might (or might not) happen with our vision statements, it is worth considering how we think of our church in contrast to the larger mission of God. If we've lost sight of our place as "mere" churches—fragile as the grass and flowers—we're well on the road toward a host of moral distortions.

Ideology universalizes the local church, making its success of cosmic importance. This heightened urgency casts a shadow over conscience and conviction, and in the name of what is "good," we will be tempted to do terrible things. Only by resisting that exchange—by recognizing that any church can be Ephesus and betray its first love—will we have the capacity to discern the circumstances, judge for ourselves, and resist the grandiosity that would make evil good and good evil.

3

Ideology, the Fall, and the Limits of Our Knowing

When Greta Gerwig's *Barbie* hit theaters, many critics and moviegoers saw echoes of Genesis 3 in the story. Barbie (played by Margot Robbie) exists in a sinless, Edenic Barbieland until one day, she has an encounter with death. That takes her out of the "garden" and into the real world. Hijinks ensue.

That interpretation makes sense, but it wasn't how the film struck me. Unlike Eden, Barbieland had a backstory. We hear of a world before Barbie, a world where women's dreams and opportunities were constrained by misogyny and patriarchy. Barbie had appeared in the world telling stories that made other visions of life plausible. Girls could be "girly" and glamorous and also win Nobel prizes or become president. In a post-Barbie world (they believed), there were no constraints on who or what a girl or woman could be or become.

In this way, Barbieland represents something that has never before been achieved in human history: utopia. But Barbie's encounter with death disrupts the utopian dream (as it does all utopian ideals). It compels her to look beyond her ideology—which means looking beyond the idealistic narratives about how we might change the world.

Barbie's makers—namely, the toy company Mattel—had spent a lifetime telling an ideological story about Barbie and believing "mission accomplished." The real world revealed a painful gap between that story and reality. The filmmakers embodied this in the contrast between Barbieland and the real world and between Robbie's Barbie and Gloria (played by America Ferrera), who is disillusioned by the challenges of life as a woman in a patriarchal world.

Seen this way, *Barbie* is the story of the failure of an ideology. It turns out that simply telling a better story did *not* change the world, and Barbie's encounter with that failure was devastating. But rather than painting this as a story of despair, we see Barbie choose life in the real world, preferring an embodied experience that promises heartache and suffering over an ideological fantasyland.

I found genius in this anti-ideological message. It managed to deconstruct without indulging in despair, offering a vision of the good life that aligns with the Beatitudes—"Blessed are those who mourn" (Matt. 5:4)—and with the Christian tradition's embrace of a tragic sense of life.

Even so, there's something interesting in comparing this story and the fall of humanity in the Scriptures, as many moviegoers did. Eve suddenly possesses knowledge she never sought; thoughts of death appear unbidden, and rather than being tempted by forbidden knowledge, she tries to cure herself of unwanted knowledge. Barbie is led to a crisis moment when she can either return to paradise or join the real world. She chooses knowledge, with its potential for the deeper joys that come from the added texture of suffering, over the blissful ignorance of Barbieland.

To root *Barbie* in Genesis 3 like this results in a somewhat abstracted, modern reading of Genesis 3—one in which the temptation of Eve and the results of her choices are more ambiguous (or in some cases, unambiguously good) than they are in the Bible's description of a fall and curse.

Knowledge and the Fall

It is inevitable that this discussion would come to Genesis 3, where the Bible tells us of the temptation of Eve and the fall of humanity. The text illuminates the evils of ideology, since ideology confronts us with a question of knowledge: what we can know and what we should know. It tempts us with forbidden fruit in the form of a key to history, promising godlike knowledge of past, present, and future.

In the dialogue between Eve and the serpent, we see seduction and distortion. This is the anatomy of temptation and the anatomy of ideology—simultaneously appealing to desire and twisting the truth.

When God planted the garden of Eden, he warned Adam not to eat of the tree of the knowledge of good and evil, "for when you eat from it you will certainly die" (Gen. 2:17). But when the serpent interrogates Eve, he asks,

> Did God really say, "You must not eat from any tree in the garden"? (3:1)

The correct response is simply, "No, he didn't say that." An even better response would be to tell the serpent to ask God, who is a regular presence in the community of the garden, or for Eve to ask God herself. But Eve chooses to respond directly, and her response contains the first signs of trouble in paradise.

> The woman said to the serpent, "We may eat fruit from the trees in the garden, but God did say, 'You must not eat fruit from the

65

tree that is in the middle of the garden, and you must not touch it, or you will die.'" (vv. 2–3)

Karl Barth calls Eve "the first religious personality"[1]—and he intends "religious" to be a negative term. She knows neither sin nor shame, but with this statement she has performed the first act of performative righteousness.

The serpent introduced a distortion, asking whether God was a miser who withheld everything good from her. Eve replied with a distortion of her own, one meant to heighten her own status. In so many words, she says, "He's only withheld one thing from us," which was the truth. But then she adds her own embellishment. "Not only have I not eaten it, I've never even touched it." In Barth's reading, the damage is already done.

> "You will not certainly die," the serpent said to the woman. "For God knows that when you eat from it your eyes will be opened, and you will be like God, knowing good and evil." (vv. 4–5)

Here, Barth calls the serpent "the first shepherd of the souls of men," offering Eve "the archetype of all sermons."[2] In it, he declares a false gospel ("You will not certainly die") and promises spiritual transformation ("You will be like God") via forbidden knowledge. It is essentially the same distortion with which the serpent began: God is a miser, withholding something good from you.

Theologian Matthew Myer Boulton develops Barth's concept of Genesis 3 as a religious experience. He describes it as "the inaugural liturgy, complete with word and sacrament"—a sermon and an invitation to the table with the devil. Boulton notes that Eve's distortion of God's command "points to one of the . . . features of not only preaching but also the whole range of verbal practices in religious life, namely, the permanent possibility, realized even in Eden, of appending merely human words to God."[3]

This is the cavalier willingness to speak on behalf of God—to wear that mantle of "rabbi" or "priest" and declare "Thus says the Lord" about something God did not say. This was uniquely unnecessary in the garden where God dwelled with them, and yet Eve acts as though God were a "distant, alien power" and the subject of "hearsay, rumor, and gossip."[4] There is no real distance, Boulton says. Yet by acting as if there were, Eve and Adam foreshadow a time when the distance will be real, when access will be cut off, and when they—not God—will be the ones absent from the garden.

This story provides us the archetype for all moral failure, including the moral failures that emerge with ideology. Here, Eve unwittingly conspires with the devil to become the first ideologue. By attributing human words to God, she has taken on God's universal perspective and dared to speak boldly about realities that are beyond her. The devil, when he speaks after her, leans into her desire for knowledge and promises to expand it.

> When the woman saw that the fruit of the tree was good for food and pleasing to the eye, and also desirable for gaining wisdom, she took some and ate it. She also gave some to her husband, who was with her, and he ate it. (v. 6)

Those consequences aren't death in the way that they (and, most likely, the original audience of Genesis) feared or anticipated. It was, instead, a terrible burden of knowledge that came crashing down on them.

> Then the eyes of both of them were opened, and they realized they were naked; so they sewed fig leaves together and made coverings for themselves. (v. 7)

67

In one sense, the serpent spoke the truth when he told them they would possess the knowledge of good and evil. But it was not knowledge like God's knowledge of evil, which is marked by holy distance. When Adam's and Eve's eyes were opened, what they saw and knew was not evil in the universal, abstract sense (as God knows it), but the specific evil that had manifest in and through them. They knew their own evil, and it filled them with shame.

Their sin would lead to their exile, and Eve's words in her dialogue with the snake almost seem to have anticipated this consequence. She articulated a righteousness based on her own merits, declaring that she'd never touched the fruit. She also acted as the guardian of the truth, as though it were her duty to answer the devil rather than turn to God. When the serpent tempted her in response, he trafficked in that desire for independence. This lie is a recapitulation of his first question, subtly accusing God "the miser" of holding back knowledge she could possess if she wanted to.

In reality, the God who forbade them from eating of the tree of knowledge was a God of mercy, and this is why Genesis 3 is critical for our discussion of ideology: it rejects one of the premises of the modern age. We assume that knowledge is always inherently good, but Adam and Eve's knowledge only produced shame.

This was indeed a revelation, but one of terrible knowledge, and a discovery that our limits—our inability to comprehend the world around us as God does—is a gift of God's mercy.

Terrible Knowledge

There are many experiences in life where we discover terrible knowledge. When my father passed away a few years ago, a friend who'd recently lost his own father said, "Life is just different after you lose your dad." I've found that to be true, and it's a knowledge I hate possessing. I imagine it's similar to what I've heard others express about the experience of losing a child.

Understood rightly, the tree of the knowledge of good and evil demonstrated God's kindness. In a perfect creation, Adam and Eve were ignorant only of terrible and tragic possibilities, which they brought into being when they ate the fruit. What we know all too well of death, suffering, loss, and grief would have remained abstractions and mysteries to them and their children.

After the fall, its results became part of life, and men and women have spent millennia trying to reckon with them in stories, practices, and religious traditions. I find it interesting that one of the consequences of modernity is the loss of many of the traditions and institutions that provided a common and cathartic encounter with grief. Between the decline of religion and the rise of nursing homes, hospitals, funeral homes, and secular cemeteries, death occurs out of view. In many remaining religious institutions, we've eschewed funerals for celebrations, believing that it is better for the soul to resist tears rather than share them.

As a result, our culture has a hard time bearing the burden of terrible knowledge. When that pent-up burden meets other factors in the modern world—ones we'll discuss later—it contributes to the eagerness with which individuals embrace ideology.

The modern age assumes that having knowledge is, in and of itself, good. Here, knowledge is simply information, and human beings are repositories of information, like computers with hard drives that can simply download information from a book or lecture.

With these assumptions in place, the fall must be reinterpreted to make the serpent a merely "complicated" character and the fall itself more a step toward enlightenment. We see this reversal reflected in popular movies such as *The Truman Show* and *The Matrix*, in which heroic figures defy their overlords in their search for truth. They must rebel in order to be free.

The aforementioned *Oppenheimer* is an interesting contrast to these stories. It certainly traffics in themes of forbidden knowledge but does so in ways that highlight the moral uncertainty of the quest. The film is based on a biography of Oppenheimer by Kai Bird and Martin J. Sherman titled *American Prometheus*. Just like in Hesiod's ancient Greek tragedy, Oppenheimer suffered after delivering "fire" to humanity.

In Hesiod's version of the tale, humanity possessed fire from the time of creation. Zeus stole it from them as an act of revenge *against Prometheus*, their maker. The two were feuding over which portions of a slaughtered ox could be given to humankind. Zeus wanted the best parts for himself, so Prometheus disguised the bones and gristle as the fattiest cuts from the belly and tricked Zeus into choosing it, allowing him to give the very best to his creation. Afterward, Zeus hid fire from humanity, and only then did Prometheus "steal" it back.

The feud wasn't over yet. Zeus's next move was to send humans a gift: Pandora's box. Until that time, human beings were mortal, but they lived long lives and didn't die. When they opened their gift from Zeus, all manner of suffering was unleashed on them: war, famine, disease, pain, and madness among them.

As Lewis Hyde points out, one of the great revelations of the story is that Zeus was actually never fooled by Prometheus:

> Prometheus fails to perceive the true meaning of the portions he so carefully arranges. To see that meaning, to see what Zeus apparently sees, it helps to know that for the Greeks the bones stand for immortality. They are the undying essence, what does not decay (they are, for example, what was preserved when the Greeks cremated a body). Conversely, in all ancient Greek literature the belly stands for needy, shameless, inexorable, overriding appetite. . . .
>
> When Zeus leaves for mortals that Promethean "better" share, mortals perforce become the very thing that they have

eaten; they become meat sacks, bellies that must be filled over and over with meat simply to delay an inexorable death. Prometheus tries to be a cunning encoder of images, but Zeus is a more cunning reader, and the meat trick backfires.[5]

This explains Zeus's final punishment of Prometheus—chaining him to a mountaintop where birds will eat his liver every day for eternity. It's an image of bottomless appetite and daily suffering. It is his curse, but also his legacy; the actual gift he gave to humankind wasn't fire but bottomless want. His failed con left him defeated and left his creation impoverished.

Prometheus spent eternity being consumed by his chastisement. Oppenheimer suffered his own humiliations years after his success at Los Alamos, eaten alive and put to shame by political rivals and the federal bureaucracy.

It's interesting to see that Nolan, Bird, and Sherman seem to get this aspect of the Prometheus myth right. In the modern age, Prometheus is often treated as a heroic, rebellious, and creative figure. The statue outside Rockefeller Center honoring Prometheus is certainly meant to convey this, and it's the way Ayn Rand thought of him. And yet, this hardly aligns with the Prometheus of ancient literature. I imagine a statue depicting *that* Prometheus—warning of the consequences of fraud and hubris—wouldn't last long at Rockefeller Center.

Taken on its original terms, the Prometheus story is a warning about what we want and what we long for. In his zeal to privilege his creations, Prometheus attempted to scam Zeus, but this con failed not only because Zeus saw through it from the beginning but because Prometheus was ignorant of what really mattered. By attempting to steal the fatty portions from the gods, he actually gave his creation hunger and want. By stoking Zeus's rage, he invited suffering—his and his creation's. It is a story that resonates far more with the underlying warnings of

Genesis 3 than with *The Matrix* or *Pleasantville*'s promises of liberation through transgression.

Past, Present, and the "Miracle of Being"

When God curses the serpent, he offers the first hint of history's redemptive arc:

> And I will put enmity
>> between you and the woman,
>> and between your offspring and hers;
> he will crush your head,
>> and you will strike his heel. (Gen. 3:15)

This prophecy is kept in ways that none of the story's cast of characters could have possibly understood. For Eve, who must have feared her own imminent death more than anything, her first foretaste of its fulfillment must have been in the reprieve she was afforded by God's provision of animal skins (a sign of a sacrifice of atonement). A second fulfillment would have come when she gave birth to her children, and yet here her story is again interrupted by grief. Her oldest son, Cain, murders her second born, Abel, but they are both lost to her because Cain is cursed to wander the earth for his crimes. Afterward, she gives birth to her son Seth, the ancestor of Noah and the rest of humanity.

Beyond these events, we know little else of her. Like most of the characters in the Scriptures, she lived life with a fairly limited grasp of the redemptive story that would be told in human history. Having experienced Eden, she knew a glory that you and I cannot imagine, and yet she could only envision the ultimate "crushing" of the serpent dimly, through the eyes of faith. Given the depths of her losses, one must imagine those eyes were familiar with tears and grief.

Her experience is typical of the way God situated his people in redemptive history. She knew the arc of that history, having experienced its origin directly and having heard the promise of a restored future. But to whatever extent she saw the events that would connect the end to the beginning, she did so as we do—"through a glass darkly" (1 Cor. 13:12 KJV).

Eve demonstrates a pattern we see throughout the Scriptures. God gives his people a story, not an ideology. He illuminates past and future but not in a way that simplifies, explains, or provides a key for interpreting them. Whether it's the Scriptures themselves or the experiences of the characters described therein, revelation has a way of both clarifying and disorienting. Like lightning at night, which can ever-so-briefly illuminate an enormous swath of landscape, revelation has a way of providing us with a tremendous amount of information and yet leaving us feeling disoriented, waiting for the next flash to confirm our next steps.

This experience is by design, of course, and not because God sadistically wants to impose limits on us. Rather, we were made for communion with him, which means we were made to be dependent on him for "daily bread"—literally and figuratively. In our covenant with him, he gives us a "lamp unto [our] feet" and a "light unto [our] path" (Ps. 119:105 KJV). These enable us to take necessary steps today, and today only.

Arendt said that ideology focuses on the past and future because it has no interest in "the miracle of being." By contrast, the Scriptures deal with the arc of history as a way of informing the present. To the extent that the Bible foretells anything about the future, whether in the prophets writing to the Jews in exile or in John the Apostle's apocalyptic visions in Revelation, it does so in broad strokes and without any ideological call to action. These prophets and revelators offer no key to history. On the contrary, the Bible makes clear time and again that redemption comes on a timetable determined by a sovereign God, and our efforts to speed up that timetable will be wasted.

Jeremiah, for instance, wrote to exiles who were divided over what to do now that they'd been dragged into captivity. Some wanted to give up on their covenant and simply assimilate among the Babylonians. (This was the purpose of the captivity, and where all the incentives lay in Babylon.) Others didn't even want to unpack their bags, certain that at any moment God might stir up a prophet and an army that would lead them back to their homeland.

Jeremiah writes to tell them something quite specific about the future—but something that is also nearly irrelevant to their personal futures. God will indeed return and rescue them, he says, but not for another seventy years (Jer. 29:10). This revelation is a double-edged sword. It's enough to help anchor their faith and hope; God hasn't abandoned them and will lead them home. But it invites grief too, because they won't experience restoration in their lifetime and aren't invited to seize power or speed up history. His audience is left with only the present to deal with, where they can choose obedience and prepare a faithful, worshiping community for his redemptive work. So the prophet tells them to settle down, start families, and be good citizens of the kingdom to which they've been taken (vv. 5–7). Their children and grandchildren, who will learn faithfulness in exile, will be the ones to whom God says:

> "For I know the plans I have for you," declares the LORD, "plans to prosper you and not to harm you, plans to give you hope and a future. Then you will call on me and come and pray to me, and I will listen to you. You will seek me and find me when you seek me with all your heart." (Jer. 29:11–13)

This passage is often treated like a Hallmark card. But Jeremiah wrote these words to disillusioned and defeated captives—literally losers in a war against the Babylonians who'd just moments before been told that they'd die in this land. It is not a promise of comfort or certainty, as many Christians hear it today; it's a tiny thread of hope offered to people who'd lost everything. These exiles are told to focus on the grief-stricken present, where they are to begin again, make peace with their captors, and learn to pray, "Come soon, Lord."

Their experience is the norm for God's people, who are never free of ambiguity and uncertainty. Abraham's journey with God was marked by his own uncertainty, which at first came from his own ambitions (fathering Ishmael when he doubted that Sarah would be able to conceive) and fear (telling Pharaoh that Sarah was his sister), and later was provoked by God calling him to do the impossible and sacrifice Isaac. At no point does Abraham know the end from the beginning; he only is given the next step, and at times—particularly before Sarah conceives—he is given long stretches of silence.

Moses makes the distinction between what can and cannot be known explicit near the end of his life. After coming within sight of the promised land, he leads the people of Israel through a covenant renewal liturgy, rehearsing their short history and celebrating the God who kept his promises to them. He ends his liturgy by admonishing them, "The secret things belong to the LORD our God, but the things revealed belong to us and to our children forever, that we may follow all the words of this law" (Deut. 29:29).

There's a lot packed into that single sentence. It begins by setting aside a black box of knowledge that we will never peer into, simply called "the secret things." But it also assures God's people that they "belong" to one who has proven himself trustworthy—Yahweh. "The LORD our God" can be trusted with possession of the secret things, as he's proven himself devoted and faithful in his love for them.

The statement also speaks positively about "things revealed." These are to be kept, remembered, and celebrated from generation to generation, and done so with a purpose—"that we may follow all the words of this law." "The secret things" and "things revealed" complement each other and work as a single declaration. There's the realm of mystery, but there is also a wealth of revelation—a story that belongs to God's people—that they must possess and preserve from generation to generation.

Put another way, Moses invites Israel to practice a twofold gesture that makes up their covenantal practice. He invites them to release the "secret things"—the uncertainties of life in a fallen world—into his hands. Then he invites them to embrace the gifts they've been given in the "revealed things"—the covenantal story and practices that are their inheritance as the children of Abraham. Together, this release and embrace serves as a shorthand for their worship and obedience.

It's an invitation that is echoed and celebrated throughout the Bible. God roots his people in a larger story, but he does not provide them with an ideology, and he rarely wants to insulate them from uncertainty or ambiguity. Instead, he wants their uncertainty to drive them to faithfulness in the present.

This lesson was difficult for Peter, a prototype for the ambitious Christian leader. Throughout Jesus's life, Peter is regularly trying to see ahead of Jesus's next steps and be the first to get involved in the action. He faces a series of humiliations, including nearly drowning while trying to walk on water, being called Satan when he rejects Jesus's prediction of his death, and being told to put away his sword in Gethsemane.

These experiences lead to his despair and denial on the night of the crucifixion, and in the final scenes of the book of John, a wiser Peter accepts a vision of his future in which he will face torture and certain death. When he looks to his friend John, he wonders, not in so many words, "If I'm going to die a wretched, tortuous death, what's going to happen to him?"

Jesus replies by asking him, "What's it to you?" The glimpse of the future he'd already been given was enough to drive him into obedience in his present, and Jesus had no interest in giving him any more.

Ideology and the Book of Job

Perhaps more than any other book of the Bible, Job most directly anticipates and confronts the evils of ideology. We associate Job with the question of theodicy—how we vindicate God in the face of evil. Why did God allow Job to suffer? Job argues that because Job is righteous, God must have gotten his facts wrong in order to allow this suffering to strike his home. His friends argue that because God is righteous, Job must have gotten his facts wrong about *himself*, and his suffering is a moral reckoning for unconfessed sins.

But Job rejects his friends' reasoning. He argues that God has acted unjustly, as though he either misunderstood or believed something false about Job's life and character. If only Job were given the opportunity, he could persuade God of his innocence.

> If only I knew where to meet him
> and could find my way to his court.
> I would argue my case before him;
> words would flow from my mouth.
> I would counter all his arguments
> and disprove his accusations.[6]

Job wants to correct the record, and he keeps appealing for God to show up so he can face him like a criminal standing trial. He's prepared his own defense as well as a prosecutor's case against God:

> He [God] does not care; so I say
> he murders both the pure and the wicked.

> When the plague brings sudden death,
> he laughs at the anguish of the innocent.[7]

Of course, God shows up, and he goes to work interrogating Job like a defendant having his day in court.

> Who is this whose ignorant words
> smear my design with darkness?
> Stand up now like a man;
> I will question you.[8]

Job is not asked about his moral righteousness at all. Instead, God asks about creation and Job's capacity for understanding. Depending on how you count them (God sometimes asks the same thing several times in a row), Job faces over sixty questions, each more perplexing than the one before.

> Do you know all the patterns of heaven
> and how they affect the earth?
> If you shout commands to the thunderclouds,
> will they rush off to do your bidding?[9]

One would think that this encounter would lead Job into rage and despair, but it doesn't. God has shifted the premises of the argument, disconnecting Job's suffering from his righteousness and situating him inside a bewildering and mysterious creation. Job is left with the only response worthy of such a revelation: worship. He responds in a litany, expressing adoration and repeating God's own words back to him (in italics):

> I know you can do all things
> and nothing you wish is impossible.
> *Who is this whose ignorant words*
> *cover my design with darkness?*
> I have spoken of the unspeakable
> and tried to grasp the infinite.[10]

In these first lines of his response, he acknowledges God's omnipotence and confesses the limits of human understanding. Unlike before, though, there is no discontentment.

> *Listen and I will speak;*
> *I will question you: please, instruct me.*
> I had heard of you with my ears;
> but now my eyes have seen you.
> Therefore I will be quiet,
> comforted that I am dust.[11]

Job has discovered the etymological origins of the word "humility," which literally comes from the word for earth or dirt (*humus*). In encountering this frailty and limits, he is strangely comforted, even in unspeakable grief.

My friend Steve Cuss refers to this as a "human-sized" sensibility. By embracing our limitations, we're freed from the anxiety that accompanies mastering our worlds and fates. It also echoes the interconnected gestures indicated by Moses in Deuteronomy 29:29, releasing what is "too great or too awesome" (Ps. 131:1 NLT) while resting in the hope and confidence of belonging to God.

It's remarkable to see what happens next in the book of Job, given his sudden speechlessness and humiliation. We might see God's rebuke as vindicating Job's friends, but he rebukes them even more harshly than he did Job:

> After he had spoken to Job, the Lord said to Eliphaz the Temanite, "I am very angry at you and your two friends, because you have not spoken the truth about me, as my servant Job has."[12]

Consider how strange this is: having just rebuked Job for questioning his justice, God now rebukes his friends for not telling the truth about him. Unlike Job, their sins are heinous enough to require atonement. God continues:

> So take seven bulls and seven rams and go to my servant Job and offer a sacrifice for yourselves. My servant Job will pray for you, and for his sake I will overlook your sin. For you have not spoken the truth about me, as my servant Job has.[13]

For good measure, we're told that they did as they were told and "the Lord accepted *Job's* prayer"[14]—meaning, God forgave them *when Job prayed for them*. This leaves us no room for doubt about who was righteous throughout the book.

To understand what they get wrong about God, we can look at two things Job seems to have gotten right.

First, Job wants to take his fight to God. Even as blasphemous ideas surge through him, he never wavers from his desire to go before God and make his case. God is not an abstraction, and Job's relationship with him isn't transactional, exchanging obedience for good will. Instead, God is personal—someone who can be argued with, confronted, and challenged. Like Jacob, Job wants to wrestle with God, and in the end, that desire is satisfied. And so is Job.

Second, Job insists that suffering is an outrage. He has the moral standing to make this case, not simply because he's lived a moral life but because through that moral life *he's come to know God*. This, more than anything else, is what distinguishes him. A chaotic, unjust world is out of line with the character of a God who loves the innocent and the meek.

Mitchell notes that Job's friends evoke God as an abstraction, a divine judge they can rationalize about. Job, meanwhile, tries to reconcile his life's circumstances with the God he knows. As Mitchell puts it:

> Any idea about God, when pursued to its extreme, becomes insanity. The idea of a just God absorbs all justice into it and

leaves a depraved creation. . . . Man becomes "that vermin, who laps up filth like water," and their god is revealed as a Stalinesque tyrant so pure that he "mistrusts his angels / and heaven stinks in his nose."[15]

In this way, Job's friends are like proto-ideologues, who took a single idea (justice) and distorted the rest of their moral universe to conform to it. Their version of God was a tyrant who related to humanity only in terms of sin and punishment, and their logic made Job out to be vermin getting what he deserved. To put it in ideological terms, God's wrath was like the process of history, marching inexorably forward to enforce absolute justice on creation. Like every ideology, this provides an explanation and a pattern with which one can make sense of the chaos and unpredictability of life. Embracing it allowed them to create a psychological distance between themselves and Job's suffering.

Job notices and makes a joke of it. "How kind you all have been to me!" he says. "How considerate of my pain!" He insists that so long as he lives, he won't buckle to their false accusations. "I will never let you convict me."[16]

The God who speaks from the whirlwind affirms Job, rejects his friends' ideology, and calls them liars. He also presents a glorious and chaotic creation that defies comprehensibility. Somehow, God has rebuked Job and yet affirmed that he has been telling the truth. Philosopher Susan Neiman explains it thus: if God is telling the truth when he presents a chaotic world, and if Job is correct to demand justice and rationality, then the story affirms humans' role as moral agents in the world. In other words, Job invites us to resist injustice: "While the book as a whole is a warning against arrogance," she writes, "it is also a reminder of the need for moral action."[17]

For those living in dark times, then, the book of Job is crucial. Most loudly, it rejects simple meaning making, whether

81

that's the ideological storytelling of Job's friends or Job's own flirtation with blasphemy when he questions God's commitment to his own principles of justice. In the end, it affirms that a world of death and suffering is not what it's meant to be, and it affirms Job's truth telling as he speaks out against it.

To seek the moral clarity of Job means accepting the tension and ambiguity that exist between what "is" and what "ought to be," advocating for the "ought" without being seduced by ideologies that offer simple, direct paths to enact it. In Job, we also have a model who didn't shy away from making a judgment about himself, his friends, or his God.

Most important, in Job we have someone who never let his experiences of suffering, grief, and personal betrayal turn him away from God—even when he thought God was among those who'd acted unjustly. His insistence on meeting with God resulted in the encounter with the whirlwind, which in turn led to his worship and his friends' atonement. Seen this way, we can say that Job's determination to take his fight to God—to struggle with him like Israel—was itself a means of bringing about a larger redemptive work.

This is critical for a church seeking renewal in dark times. Job knew what the disciples knew who watched many others wander off when confronted with difficult words. "To whom shall we go? You have the words of eternal life" (John 6:68).

Ideology and the Scriptures

I'm tempted to keep going with these biblical examples. One could also fill books unpacking Paul's references to mysteries revealed and unrevealed or to the "hiddenness" of the Christian life. Themes of God's providence and sovereignty could also serve as a springboard to talk about the folly of comprehensibility. Or one could simply look at the life of Jesus and the way he cleverly managed revelation in order to carry out his mission on his own timeline. But I'm hoping that if you're not already convinced, you'll take the issue to the Scriptures for yourself. I'm confident that those authors will do a far better job than I can to argue for limits of human understanding.

So instead, let me return to the power of ideology. In particular, I want to talk about how ideology distorts the Scriptures.

I would love to imagine that simply presenting a committed believer with the words of the Bible would be enough to persuade them, but that isn't how people or texts work. Each of us has an interpretive framework formed by the ideas (and ideologies) we encounter, our own habits of reading and thinking, and an untold number of practices and experiences. So every text we encounter, biblical and otherwise, is read through that framework and whatever distorting effects it may have.

To that end, there are two examples of ideological reactions to the Scriptures that I think about regularly; they exemplify how truly and terribly things can go wrong.

The first is a story I heard Russell Moore, editor in chief of *Christianity Today* (and, full disclosure, my boss), tell several years ago. He shared it in his most recent book:

> Pastor after pastor has described for me almost identical experiences in which they would parenthetically quote, somewhere in a sermon, a statement along the lines of "turn the other cheek," only to be met after the service with irate church members demanding to know where they had gotten the "liberal talking points." At first, I chalked up such controversies to biblical illiteracy. . . . Instead, though, often the angry Christians knew exactly who had said those words. As one congregant said to his pastor, "We've tried the 'turn the other cheek' stuff. It doesn't work. It's time now to fight." We have arrived at the point at which, for many people who name the name of Jesus Christ, Christlikeness is compromise. How did this happen?[18]

If I could be bold enough to answer his question, I would simply say, "ideology." This is a textbook case of political ideology's logic distorting a Christian's moral theology, enabling them to reject the teaching of Jesus in the name of a culture war they believe they're fighting on behalf of Christianity.

Of course, political ideology is kind of low-hanging fruit, so another example bears inclusion. This one has nothing to do with politics, coming instead from a contemporary worship song written in 2004.

We introduced Tim Hughes's "You" at a worship service sometime that year, and it quickly joined the other British imports that were part of our church's catalog of songs. One Sunday after a service, a small gaggle of members and regular attenders made their way to the front of the church as I wrapped cables and chatted with other members of our worship ministry.

As a worship leader, you develop a certain radar for trouble. During the service, it helps you spot the guy who is about to rush the stage with the tambourine he just pulled from his backpack, and it helps you notice when a new worship leader has locked her knees and is about to black out. After the service, it helps you notice when you're about to get a lecture. That particular alarm went off this evening. Maybe it was the body language or the huge Bible with Post-it flags poking out at chaotic angles.

In any case, these concerned citizens wanted to address a problem with the second half of the chorus of "You":

> Who can know the mind of God? / Who can
> understand Your ways?
> And these words are not enough / To tell of Your great
> name.

To these folks, these verses contradicted Scripture. We can, they argued, of course know the mind of God from the Bible.

84

Between the three or four of them, they each had an angle from which they were concerned about the text: it belittled Scripture, it might discourage Christians from trying to understand difficult truths, it was flirting with mysticism ("which starts with mist and ends in schism"), and so on.

The problem, of course, was that the chorus in question was a near-direct quote of Romans 11:33–36:

> Oh, the depth of the riches of the wisdom and
> knowledge of God!
> How unsearchable his judgments,
> and his paths beyond tracing out!
> "Who has known the mind of the Lord?
> Or who has been his counselor?"
> "Who has ever given to God,
> that God should repay them?"
> For from him and through him and for him are all things.
> To him be the glory forever! Amen.

When I pointed this out, they acknowledged the point, but noted that a passage like this shouldn't be read without careful explanation. We don't want to give people the wrong impression, as though the Christian life contained experiences that couldn't be explained, or as if God's will couldn't be known through his Word.

To put it another way, the problem with the verse (and, of course, the song itself) was that it needed to be run through the iron logic of an ideology that promised a comprehensible world. And rather than confront that ideology with the words of God, they preferred either to explain that it didn't mean what it plainly said or to sing something else entirely.

The point in revisiting this decades-old argument is simply to point out that this sort of thing happens all the time. Ideology demands that reality conform to our ideas, that facts bend to their abstract logic. If what we observe or experience contradicts the key to history, an explanation must be manufactured that causes everything to fit.

This example is a mostly harmless one, but you can imagine more dangerous iterations. When a community has come to believe that their mission is to change the world and that God has uniquely gifted their leader to bring that change into existence, an encounter with an unpleasant fact—the leader's mistreatment of staff or an inappropriate sexual relationship—cannot be allowed to disrupt the mission. Instead, reality itself must bend, and thus a story must be manufactured and strictly maintained that either justifies their actions, blames the victims, or gives moral license to the leader. This isn't just for the sake of the leader or the mission; it's also for the sake of the followers. Their world's coherence and consistency are at stake too, and they want to guard that stability as fiercely as anyone.

4

Authority, Violence, and the Erosion of Meaning

> Our chief weapon is surprise . . . surprise and fear . . . fear and surprise. . . . Our two weapons are fear and surprise . . . and ruthless efficiency. . . . Our *three* weapons are fear, and surprise, and ruthless efficiency . . . and an almost fanatical devotion to the Pope. . . . Our *four* . . . no . . . *amongst* our weapons. . . . Amongst our weaponry are such elements as fear, surprise. . . . I'll come in again.
>
> —Monty Python's Cardinal Ximinez[1]

On October 31, 1992, Pope John Paul II tried to right a wrong. Years before, a Christian who had never denied his faith or challenged the church's creeds had found himself under a cloud of suspicion. As a result, he was blocked from teaching at universities and cut off from academic and social life—literally placed under house arrest—for the rest of his life. John Paul II wanted to correct a "tragic mutual misunderstanding,"[2] acknowledging that church officials had gotten this one wrong.

It's an interesting speech. It pays homage to the work and integrity of the falsely accused, but I'm not sure it sufficiently accounts for the suffering inflicted on the victim. Nonetheless, I'm sure he would have appreciated the gesture, had he still been alive. But of course, by then, Galileo Galilei had been dead for 350 years.

As we reviewed in chapter 2, Arendt was interested in how Galileo's contributions gave rise to a "universal perspective" and our modern sense of comprehensibility. But we shouldn't be too quick to move past his story. It's the story of a brilliant scientist and craftsman whose discoveries changed the world; it's also the story of a Christian whose great sin was telling the truth despite church authority and power.

The details of that conflict, and the fallout that reshaped Christendom in its aftermath, are worth examining. For those who've studied or experienced conflict and crisis in evangelical life firsthand, some of it will be all too familiar.

Revolutions

When Galileo first published *The Starry Messenger*, his predecessor Copernicus's work wasn't considered heretical or forbidden. A few warned that Copernican theory contradicted the Scriptures. But because Copernicus's work was abstract in nature and didn't attempt to explain how the world appeared, it was considered harmless enough. By contrast, *The Starry Messenger* erupted into heresy trials and threats of torture and worse. What made them different?

There are two answers to that question. The first, as articulated by Arendt, is found in chapter 2: Galileo's findings would change how we see and experience the world. The second answer is more subtle, a topic Arendt often covers though not necessarily with regard to Galileo: his claims undermined the church's authority. The two ideas are interrelated. To understand them, we must briefly go back to Copernicus.

Today we accept that the abstract language of math can truthfully describe natural phenomena. Consider $E = mc^2$. We take the familiar equation as a truth claim—to calculate the amount of energy (E) in an object, multiply its mass (M) times the speed of light (C) squared. If someone announced that they'd used a mathematical model to unlock, say, the origins of COVID or to end the chaos at airports, we'd accept it as such. We would be inclined to accept math as a useful tool in the search for truth.

That wasn't assumed in the time of Copernicus. This isn't to say that Copernicus avoided persecution because "math is hard" (though I'm sure that played a factor). Rather, it simply didn't hold pride of place as a source of truth just yet.

Galileo's findings bridged the gap between abstraction and experience. One didn't need to understand algebra to confirm his findings. You just needed decent vision and a telescope. The device did the rest of the work in reshaping the way you saw the world.

Among the things affected by the collision of theory and senses was language. Common language and biblical language describing the world as "firmly established" and "unmoving"[3] or the sun as "rising and setting"[4] was, according to Galileo, not literally true. Some church officials accepted these passages as poetic metaphors, while others saw such an understanding as an affront to the Bible's claims of being God-breathed. Some also thought that it set a terrible precedent to let discoveries from the natural sciences challenge the authoritative interpretations of the church.

The church chose to hold fast to geocentrism, subjecting Galileo to the Inquisition. He was found both wrong and heretical—a damnable offense.

This infuriated Galileo. In a letter that holds up to this day, he described how the church was demanding literalism out of passages of Scripture that were never intended to be read literally. In forcing the Bible to say what it didn't say, it made the church look ridiculous, defending their arguments for falsehoods. "These men have resolved to fabricate a shield for their fallacies out of the mantle of pretended religion and the authority of the Bible," he wrote. "These they apply, with little judgment, to the refutation of arguments that they do not understand and have not even listened to."[5]

In 1616, heliocentrism was officially condemned as heresy. Galileo was called to Rome and warned to no longer teach on the subject—a command he obeyed until 1632, when he published a second book, *Two Chief World Systems*. The book expanded on the arguments in *The Starry Messenger*. Once again, he was called before the Inquisition, this time forced to recant his teaching under threat of torture. He did but was nonetheless sentenced to house arrest where he remained— largely cut off from family, friends, and social life—until his death a decade later.

Nearly four hundred years later, what happened to Galileo seems comically absurd. The church simply didn't understand the times. Perhaps a century earlier, the Inquisition's efforts to suppress Galileo might have succeeded, but by this time, the Protestant Reformation was in full swing, and its ethos emboldened Galileo and his allies. Even more significant was another trend—one that also fueled the Reformation and the scientific revolution: the printing press and a rise in literacy.

In the fifteenth century when the Gutenberg press was first invented, only about 10 percent of Europeans could read. By the seventeenth century, nearly half of all Europeans could read. *The Starry Messenger* was a bestseller in its day, copied and distributed widely. Like scientific papers today, the publication of his theories and methods made his work repeatable. Anyone with a telescope (which were becoming more widely available all the time) could "check his work," which meant that the church wasn't simply attempting to suppress one man's ideas; it was soon at war against a legion.

The replicability of Galileo's work gave birth to the age of science and, in many ways, to modern thought itself. But it would be incorrect to credit him with the rise of secularism as such. For Galileo, there was no tension between the sciences and religion, so long as the church was willing to hold its authority over interpretation as subordinate to the authority of the Scriptures themselves. In other words, of course the Scriptures were infallible and God-breathed, but should our understanding of them be confronted by new challenges such as those emerging from the natural sciences, church leaders ought to practice humility and curiosity and entertain new interpretations.

Of course, church leaders didn't see it this way. Their coercive response—rather than Galileo's teaching as such—is the very thing that destroyed their credibility and authority in the years to come.

Galileo and Spiritual Abuse

I confess that Galileo took me by surprise as I was working on this book. I knew before I sat down to write it that he'd make an appearance; the impact of his work was already a part of the larger story I wanted to tell. But as I looked at him closely for the first time in decades, I saw a familiar pattern: a Christian publicly humiliated, their salvation questioned, their livelihood crushed, and their social connections severed at the hands of the church. All for having told an uncomfortable truth.

It's true that Galileo ultimately won the debate both inside the church and out. Even the pope is a heliocentrist now. On the day after Pope John Paul II gave the speech honoring him, a *New York Times* headline read, "It's Official: The Earth

Revolves around the Sun, Even for the Vatican." But none of that diminishes what Galileo endured—years spent under threat of torture, a decade in physical confinement and isolation, the public humiliation, the dismissal of his life's work as anti-Christian. When he died in 1642, his family and patrons conspired to quickly and quietly bury him at the Basilica at Santa Croce, concerned that the Inquisition would deny him a consecrated, Christian burial. He lay there for ninety-five years before his remains were moved into a marked tomb built in his honor.

I knew Galileo mattered if we wanted to understand how the modern world came to be; I never thought of him as a victim of spiritual abuse.

That label "spiritual abuse" gets tossed around a lot these days, and one could be excused for feeling like it's a bit of a catchall. It is equally applied to accusations of financial misconduct, narcissistic behavior, sexual abuse, and general meanness from Christian leaders, and I confess that I've often been wary of using it. It's much like the word "trauma"— a word and experience that I consider deeply significant to the concerns of pastoral theology in the twenty-first century. If everything is trauma or if every ugly behavior is spiritual abuse, I fear we lose the ability to rightly and specifically name experiences of great significance. Allowing these words to be used too liberally actually works in favor of abusive leaders; they can shrug and say, "Everything is spiritual abuse these days."

Defining the term is essential, then, but presents challenges of its own. The trouble with defining the term is that it must be broad enough to include a variety of behaviors (including many of those listed above) and specific enough to resist being a catchall.

I've found two definitions particularly helpful. They both make it a point to distinguish spiritual abuse from other kinds—

such as physical, sexual, or emotional—though they also ac-knowledge that the lines between these can be blurred. The first, from Michael Kruger, locates its defining characteristic in its ends:

> Spiritual abuse, then, is when a spiritual leader—such as a pastor, elder, or head of a Christian organization—wields his position of spiritual authority in such a way that he manipu-lates, domineers, bullies, and intimidates those under him, as a means of accomplishing what he takes to be biblical and/or spiritual goals.[6]

The second, from Diane Langberg, focuses on the subject and impact of abuse:

> The word spiritual refers to something affecting a human spirit or soul. Abuse means to mistreat another, to deceive or do harm. When we use the word spiritual to describe abuse, we are talking about using that which is sacred—including God's Word—to control, misuse, deceive, or damage a person created in his image.[7]

Kruger's definition provides the architecture of spiritual abuse. It requires an element of spiritual authority—whether explicit or implied—and operates with spiritual goals in mind. The latter is a critical element of this issue. Spiritual abuse often goes unrecognized because it fits within a rubric of authority and purpose. A pastor's abusive behavior will be tolerated for much longer if there are noble "ends" to point to: the church is growing, evangelistic ministry is booming, young people are showing up.

On the other hand, Langberg (as she always does) brings things down to the level of persons made in the image of God, individuals who will bear the scars of abuse for the rest of their lives.

Taken together—the architecture and the individual—the whole picture becomes clear. Spiritual abuse leverages a victim's deepest beliefs to coerce them in service of a person, group, or institution.

That coercion can take many forms, including physical, emotional, or sexual abuse. It can also aim to gain control over a person's finances, relationships, or vocational decisions. Whatever the case, spiritual abuse robs a person of agency, depending on *their* spiritual commitments to be strong enough to compel obedience or submission.

That's a frightening thing to read—at least I hope it is. It hopefully bears the marks of James 3:1, where the apostle warns that pastors are judged more harshly, or Matthew 18:6, where Jesus warns that anyone who causes one of his little ones to stumble will sleep with the fish.

Many pastors I know feel that weight, and they feel the tension and anxiety of a cultural moment when they are under scrutiny in new ways. They fear being called a "narcissist," but they also fear being lax in their responsibility to pastor the people under their care and speak boldly when needed. It feels like an impossible task. More than one have joked, "Please don't make a podcast about me."

I would argue, though, that this conversation about spiritual abuse is beginning at the wrong end of the story. We see spiritual devastation after a pastoral failure and ask, How can I avoid that? How can I protect myself, or protect my church? The answer lies way upstream from these events—in decisions that were made years before the catalytic events that actually led to public humiliation and failure.

As I've considered these questions, I keep tracing the problem back to one issue in particular: authority. If we misunderstand the nature of authority, how it *operates*, how it collapses, and the healthy limits with which it exists in human relationships (and the church in particular), we're bound to stumble into disaster. The Galileo affair is itself an example of a church mishandling a crisis of authority on the grandest scale. Its missteps are prototypical of many of the church leadership crises we've witnessed in the past two decades.

To understand them, we need to begin with another fundamental question: What is authority? And to answer it, once again we turn to our companion throughout this book.

Arendt and Authority

According to Arendt, from the moment we ask, "What is authority?" we are in trouble. "We are tempted and entitled to raise this question because authority has vanished from the modern world," she writes. "Little about its nature appears self-evident or even comprehensible to everybody, except that the political scientist may still remember that this concept was once fundamental to political theory, or that most will agree that a constant, ever-widening and -deepening crisis of authority has accompanied the development of the modern world in our century."[8]

The trouble begins much earlier than our century, actually, and it exists in part because authority—of the sort that Arendt admires—is historically a rare thing. For her, it describes a relationship between rulers (or leaders) and ruled (or followers) marked by "an obedience in which men retain their freedom." This can be confusing, she acknowledges: "Since authority always demands obedience, it is commonly mistaken for some form of power or violence. Yet authority precludes the use of external means of coercion; where force is used, authority itself has failed."[9]

Put another way, authority evokes obedience without pressure or threat of violence. But what can possibly achieve this?

To answer that question, we can contrast authority with two familiar alternatives: *tyranny*, the rule of the one, and *authoritarianism*, the rule of the few. In tyranny, there is no functional distinction between the will of the leader and the law. In authoritarianism, power is vested in the laws, codes, and rules—written or unwritten—that establish the community. The law is brutally enforced, and power is absolute among those who possess the power of the state. The common thread between them is the absence of freedom. Obedience is motivated primarily by the threat of consequences for disobedience, which in either case can be limitless.

By contrast, authority is a positive motivation. One obeys an authority in the interest of something greater, whether that's for religious reasons, a vision of common good, or deeply held beliefs.

For Arendt, the best historical example of authority is the Roman Republic. For its citizens, the source of authority in Rome wasn't Caesar or his military. It was Rome itself, its citizens, and most importantly, the *idea* of Rome and the powerful sense of participation in the story and tradition flowing from its founding.[10] "Contrary to our concept of growth," Arendt writes, "where one grows into the future, the Romans felt that growth was directed toward the past."[11] They "felt they needed founding fathers and authoritative examples in matters of thought and ideas as well, and accepted the great 'ancestors' in Greece as their authorities for theory, philosophy, and poetry. The great Greek authors became authorities in the hands of the Romans, not of the Greeks."[12]

This understanding of authority took visible shape in the structure of the republic, but it also existed in the culture of deference to tradition. That cultural thread is what was preserved after the collapse of the republic and the rise of Octavian, who remade Rome as an empire (which is to say, a tyranny). It was reinvigorated and reinvented with the conversion of Constantine in the fifth century. That was when the church "was able to overcome the anti-political and anti-institutional tendencies of the Christian faith, which had caused so much trouble in earlier centuries, and which are so manifest in the New Testament and in early Christian writings and seemingly so insurmountable."[13] What emerged was a redefinition of what it meant to be Roman, with a new founding located in the origins of Christianity, a new tradition in the life and practice of faith, and new "founding fathers" located in the apostles and early church fathers.

The church's authority took hold in part because of genuine religious fervor, in part because of the order of the emperor, and in part by its leaders' own claims of apostolic succession—their assertion that they were the only true guardians of the faith. In doing this, Arendt says, the church "adopted the Roman distinction between authority and power, claiming for herself the old authority of the Senate and leaving the power—which in the Roman Empire was no longer in the hands of people but had been monopolized by the imperial household—to the princes of the world."[14]

This became the status quo for the Western world for more or less a millennium, until Martin Luther sparked the Protestant Reformation. About a century after that, Galileo would build his telescope.

Eternal Punishment and Coercion

As Arendt readily admits, no authority—not even the Roman Republic—existed without some measure of coercion. Starting with Plato, the question of authority always operated on a kind of two-track basis. One track was for those in the high culture of the city—philosophers, religious leaders, statesmen, and those otherwise able to participate. For them, Plato made the positive arguments of his political philosophy. These privileged few could pursue beauty through contemplation and make it manifest in the world through speech and action.

The second track was for everyone else, those who for what-ever reason couldn't or wouldn't participate, or those for whom a positive vision of the good life wasn't sufficient to constrain bad behavior and bad impulses. For these, Plato wrote the con-cluding myths of *The Republic*, describing an afterlife where punishments and rewards were based on what you did in this life. Arendt doesn't use the word herself, but I think it's cor-rect to say that she saw this as a *cynical* move by Plato, "an ingenious device to enforce obedience upon those who are not subject to the compelling power of reason, without actually using external violence."[15]

For Arendt, these were written for purely political purposes and meant to be used by "the few" to control the worst impulses of "the many" who wouldn't be taking part in the life of the philosopher, which is to say, those who weren't part of the rul-ing class. This vision of hell, she argues, is what appears later in Christianity. She writes:

> The introduction of the Platonic hell into the body of Chris-tian dogmatic beliefs strengthened religious authority to the point where it could hope to remain victorious in any con-test with secular power. But the price paid for this additional strength was that the Roman concept of authority was diluted, and an element of violence was permitted to insinuate itself into both the very structure of Western religious thought and the hierarchy of the Church. . . . As far as religious thought is concerned, it certainly is a terrible irony that the "glad tidings" of the Gospels, "Life is everlasting," should eventu-ally have resulted not in an increase of joy but of fear on earth, should not have made it easier but harder for man to die.[16]

Here, I must disagree and yet agree with Arendt. On one hand, it's far too sweeping to suggest that hell was a political myth invented by Plato and imported into Christian doctrine out of political necessity. Jesus himself described visions of hell, and the Old Testament's vision of Sheol predates him.

On the other hand, the doctrine of hell can play a powerful coercive role in establishing church authority. And Arendt is right to call our attention to the role that hell played in establishing the church's power and influence in the post-Constantinian world. Not only was the church the source of the good news about the life, death, and resurrection of Jesus; it also dictated participation in forgiveness and resurrection. Galileo's story illustrates that monopoly too. He didn't just fear the physical and psychological torture that the Inquisition might inflict on him; he feared the consequences of being denied the Eucharist, his last rites, and a Christian burial. In other words, the church wasn't just threatening to humiliate him and inflict untold pain on him; it could deny his entrance to heaven.

Evangelicals would vigorously deny that the sacraments of the church provide assurance of entry to heaven or hell. But evangelical theology maintains that the church (and often pastors in particular) plays a role in confirming or assuring Christians that their confession of faith is authentic. Churches that practice formal church discipline do so with this concept in mind, believing that they have a duty to put the fear of God in wayward members, excommunicating them when they feel that their lack of repentance makes them no longer able to rest assured in their salvation.

The result is only different by degrees from the role of the Catholic Church in administering or denying a person the Eucharist. This is why James 3:1 warns the church that pastors will be judged more strictly. All churches that practice any measure of church discipline and excommunication hold a spectacular coercive power.

The unjust exercise of that power is at the heart of the Galileo affair. The result was destructive for Galileo, but it was also destructive for the church. They reacted to his teaching with violence, manifest as the destruction of Galileo's good name and his confinement, cutting him off from the common world. They also maintained a looming threat of physical violence.

In other words, they lied about him and made him an outcast, hoping that his example would dissuade others from contradicting the church's official teaching. It worked for a time but only in dissuading *public* support for Galileo.

Arendt writes, "Violence destroys that which it was meant to save." A leader or institution only reaches for it when efforts to persuade fail. But once you've reached for violence, true authority has vanished. The notion that the church could simply be taken at its word when making a claim for the truth could no longer be trusted. Descartes, for instance, writing in 1635, hoped that the church would back away from labeling heliocentrism a heresy, but he acknowledged that even if it didn't, "I would continue to believe it to be true." For him, the damage to its leaders' authority and the impossibility of simply taking them at their word was already an established fact.

Descartes would later be among the first to recommend that the church delineate and limit its claim on authority to "matters of faith," leaving "the study of nature to scientists." Shortly after that, he published *Discourse on Method*, which was a far more aggressive assault on the church's authority than anything Galileo or Copernicus ever wrote.

In punishing Galileo, the church destroyed the possibility of its being part of the larger conversation of science and knowledge in the modern era.

Bundled Identity

In the upheaval of the next five hundred years, the human experience would be fundamentally transformed. There were the technological, social, and political changes of the Enlightenment, but also deeper psychological and spiritual transformations, shifting the way we understood ourselves and our world.

Imagine, for example, someone born in Trier, Germany, a little before 1500—just at the edge of the Reformation and scientific revolution. He is a middle-class citizen of the Holy Roman Empire. His family is Catholic. His father is a butcher, and so he will be too. Shortly after he was born, his parents arranged for him to marry the baker's daughter.

Within that sketch, we see his nationality, his class, his vocation, his family, and his religious commitments. And barring some dramatic disruption, they will not change until the day he dies. Not only that, the thought of changing religions, moving to some faraway place, or climbing a social ladder will never even cross his mind.

He has what philosopher Charles Taylor calls a "bundled identity."[17] These attributes come to him like a birthright, and nothing in the ordinary circumstances of his world will break them apart.

For instance, imagine if he were drawn into practices like black magic and divination. His thinking about witchcraft will always be contested by deeper, more rooted conceptions of the world that were shaped by his Catholicism, citizenship, and family. These are his default setting, rooted in the institutions that shape his world—the monarchy, the church, and the family.

It's helpful to imagine these identifying characteristics like the branches of a root system. Each one—nation, family, religion, vocation—stretches toward an institution that feeds those roots, shaping the person who grows up out of them.

Above the soil is the rest of the world. It's where a person encounters the natural world, pursues their vocation, practices their religion, and interacts with other people. Five hundred years ago, there was a deeply embedded sense of mystery, uncertainty, and transcendence in that world. When a person stood outside and stared into the darkness, they sensed something much more imposing and overwhelming than we do. Rainstorms, failed crops, sickness, and mental illness were attributed to supernatural forces—the work of evil spirits, the alignment of the planets, or divine retribution.

Taylor describes this world as "enchanted," a place full of meaning, mystery, and uncertainty. A person had a sense of vulnerability[18] to unseen realities—angels and demons, good and bad luck, blessings and curses, magic, and prayer.

At that time, a Christian faced many of the doubts we all do, but as Taylor puts it, it would be "virtually impossible"[19] for someone in this world to *not* believe in God. This results not from a conscious choice between belief and unbelief but from an intuitive "feel of the world" or "cosmic imaginary"[20] shaped by the stories and practices that they'd heard all their life. In this way, the world felt open to transcendence and mystery, and their imagination had wings to explore it.

These elements—roots and wings—fed into one another. From the roots came the stories and traditions that shaped a way of seeing the world that was open to transcendence, and from a winged imagination came the experiences that provided meaning and reinforced a person's connection with their rooting institutions.

Unbundled Identity

Now, every aspect of identity that defined the life of the butcher's son is fundamentally changed. The Protestant Reformation gave space for individuals to question their religious commitments and sever ties to religious authorities. Once this kind of spiritual conversion became a possibility, it opened the door to others. Today, one might change religions at any point in life, and you might do it many times. You might become an atheist, a member of an alien abduction cult, a fundamentalist, a Buddhist, or an Episcopalian, and for the most part people won't bat an eye.

At the same time that this spiritual and religious transformation was unfolding, the scientific revolution took off. The idea that storms and rain were attributable to the wrath or blessing of God began to unravel once French scientist Pierre Gassendi and Italian physicist Evangelista Torricelli made sense of air temperature and condensation. Antonie van Leeuwenhoek saw his "little animals," which led to the discovery of bacteria and germs and displaced the role of demons and curses as causes of disease. When Sigmund Freud pioneered psychotherapy, he was able to help his patients understand that the voices in their heads were not demons; they were just their mothers.

This revolution effectively clipped our wings and left us with a "disenchanted"[21] world. In place of open skies and a sense of mystery and uncertainty came what Taylor calls the "immanent frame"[22]—a barrier where, unprompted by anything but ourselves, thoughts about transcendence or spirituality bump their heads. Where five hundred years ago it was unthinkable to not believe in God, today, particularly among elite communities and institutions, it is belief that seems nearly unthinkable.

Other developments mirrored the effect of the Reformation on identity. The Industrial Revolution and invention of mass transit weakened our bonds to place. Economic and social changes created opportunities for individuals to move up or down the social ladder; the butcher's kid might be a banker or a teacher or the president of the United States. Political revolutions literally dethroned monarchies and broke up empires.

Today, the world is a freer, more democratic, more prosperous place than ever before in human history. We now have the freedom to pursue happiness in love, in work, and in choosing where and how to live, but that freedom was hard-won. As Jonah Goldberg says, human nature is inherently tribal and hostile to outsiders.[23] To achieve a world of pluralism and freedom is something of a miracle. But it comes at a cost.

Where the butcher's son was born with strong connecting roots to institutions that provided stories and meaning to his life, our roots are weak and brittle, subject to being severed at a moment's notice. The institutions they connect us to are a shell of what they once were, having lost much of their authority and influence because of scandal, superfluousness, or the loss of the transcendent beliefs that once gave them meaning.

The resulting "unbundled" identity is marked by anxiety and uncertainty. Having the freedom to choose what we believe, where we live, what we do, and who we marry is both liberating—we're free to choose for ourselves—and burdensome—we *have* to choose for ourselves. To put it another way, each of these identity characteristics is a question we now have to answer—and not just once. We may spend a lifetime making choices about who we want to be, calling them into question, and having to choose again. And again.

Underneath all these questions, driving the others to the surface, is a deeper uncertainty: *What gives my life meaning?* The answer to this question evades us because of the loss of our roots and wings. When we're cut off from institutions that provide meaning-filled stories or when those institutions have lost the credibility to tell them, it leaves our spiritual imagination impoverished. In the moments when we do venture to pray or worship or try to envision meaning or connection to the supernatural, we'll find our thoughts bumping up against the ceiling of the immanent frame.

We're left to look for meaning *within immanence*, and those efforts typically leave us wanting. Taylor calls it the "malaise of immanence," a melancholy that appears along with "the eclipse of transcendence."[24] He writes:

> We can feel this emptiness in the everyday, but also it comes out with particular force in what should be the crucial moments of life: birth, marriage, death. . . .

But we can also just feel the lack in the everyday. This can be where it most hurts. This seems to be felt particularly by people of some leisure and culture. For instance, some people sense a terrible flatness in the everyday, and this experience has been identified particularly with commercial, industrial, or consumer society. They feel the emptiness of the repeated, accelerating cycle of desire and fulfillment in consumer culture; the cardboard quality of bright supermarkets, or neat row housing in a clean suburb; the ugliness of slag heaps, or an aging industrial townscape.[25]

Solving that malaise is the central preoccupation of much of our culture. Whether it's the pseudo-spirituality of self-help, enthused participation in religious communities, political activism, consumerism, obsession with youth and beauty, mindless entertainment, or endless consumption, we are looking for something to cling to that makes us feel satisfied physically, sexually, or materially. We want to be seen and welcomed or blessed, and the world offers us a thousand ways to do it. None of them work, of course, because we're rootless people. Any successes or achievements will soon enough be met with new expressions of dissatisfaction. We will turn again to our compressed reality and continue the search.

To put this in an explicitly Christian framework, we know we're meant to find meaning and purpose in relationship with God. Our fallen world presents a thousand obstacles to that relationship, and in a secular age the "malaise of immanence" is among the most powerful. We struggle to encounter God (and meaning and purpose) because all thoughts about the transcendent and supernatural are hampered, and this sends us searching within immanence. We want a story or a sense of belonging that will fill the void left by being cut off from transcendent experience. It is precisely this desire, and the expectation that it can be met within the immanent world, that prepares the souls of men and women for ideological evil.

Loneliness

I've chosen Taylor's way of telling this story because of his focus on religion and secularism, but Arendt offers a similar account of modernity's effect on the human experience. Hers is more narrowly focused on the political and social impact, however, though she arrives at a similar understanding of the erosion of meaning and identity.

As a result, she says, three phenomena begin to take hold of men and women: uprootedness, superfluousness, and ultimately, loneliness.

She describes uprootedness as having "no place in the world."[26] Superfluousness emerges as a result of the Industrial Revolution, where work has been transformed, systematized, and standardized. In the factory, men and women become cogs in a machine, trained for repetitive, menial tasks, and are easily replaced.

Uprootedness and superfluousness are the fertile soil from which loneliness emerges. Arendt argues that this, more than anything else, primes a person for "totalitarian domination" or, in our case, captivity to totalizing ideology.[27] Such loneliness isn't mere solitude or isolation,[28] since one can be perfectly happy in solitude or miserable in a crowd.

Solitude is an essential part of human flourishing, a spiritually rich environment that is the primary space for thinking. Arendt describes it as a place where the individual becomes two-in-one, which is to say that it's a place where we participate in a dialogue with ourselves. Only through this self-interrogation and testing of our ideas are we able to discern what we think or to make a judgment.

For solitude to be rich and useful, it requires a community to which one returns. This is essential for two reasons. First, community is the place where the thoughts that emerged in solitude are tested in conversations with others. Second, community is where the two-in-one "becomes whole" again, a person with ideas and judgments in relationship with others.

Loneliness, however, never requires solitude and isn't alleviated with the presence of a crowd. Arendt calls it "the experience of not belonging to the world at all, which is among the most radical and desperate experiences of man."[29] This rootlessness is the bridge to loneliness. The brittle or broken bonds of identity offer no sense of self, and when isolated, a person doesn't find the two-in-one of solitude but rather a one-in-one. There is no conversation partner.

Life in the compressed world is lonely too. Disenchanted people who lack unifying principles are atomized, anxious, and desperate for meaning. This makes them ideal prey for possession by Dostoyevsky's demons—tyrannical ideas that will consume them.

The power of ideology is in its logical consistency "from which there is no escape."[30] When you are alone in your head—lonely in your head—incapable of the two-in-one dialogue of solitude, ideology makes a compelling conversation partner. It's always repeating the simple premise again and again, promising that unwavering faithfulness to its central idea will one day bring about peace of balance, or it might restore a long-gone sense of pride.

Ideology by nature tends toward the extreme, and loneliness accelerates the process. Arendt, quoting Luther, writes, "A lonely man . . . 'always deduces one thing from the other and thinks everything to the worst.'" This, combined with the extremism of ideology, always leads to "the worst possible conclusions."[31]

Together, you can see a developmental process for ideological evil: disenchantment and rootlessness produce loneliness. Loneliness produces an anxious search for meaning. The church, to the extent she retains a voice in our world, has lost authority due to her own indulgence of violence and coercion.

Ideology is left as a compelling source of meaning without many challengers. With its elegant simplicity and iron logic, it both seduces and traps followers, and it is incredibly difficult to break its grip.

5

Discovering the Banality of Evil

At 8:05 p.m. on May 11, 1960, Ricardo Klement got off the bus after a long day of work at the Mercedes Benz company in Buenos Aires. He began walking home when a man approached him and asked in Spanish, "Do you have a moment?" Immediately, two other men appeared and leapt on him, wrestling him to the ground and stuffing him into the back of a car. They weren't two-bit thugs though; they were agents of Israel's Mossad.

They bound Klement's hands and feet, put blackout goggles over his eyes, and gagged him, pushing him out of sight on the floorboards to ensure no one saw them as they drove to a safe house. Argentina had no extradition treaty with Israel, so all of this was highly illegal. Nonetheless, nine days later, they dressed him in an El Al Airlines uniform, drugged him nearly senseless, and, under the ruse that he was recovering from a head injury, flew him to Israel.

Israel's Prime Minister David Ben-Gurion announced the capture to the world on May 23, using his real name: Adolf Eichmann, the Nazi war criminal. Eichmann, he said, was responsible along with other Nazi leaders for what they called the final solution to the Jewish problem, that is, the extermination of the six million Jews of Europe. Adolf Eichmann is already under arrest in Israel and will soon face trial in Israel, in keeping with the laws governing justice for the Nazis and their helpers.[1]

By then, Arendt was a world-renowned political thinker. She'd written the definitive book on totalitarianism shortly after the war and had published *The Human Condition*, her book of political theory, in 1958. She was a regular contributor to mainstream US periodicals like *The Atlantic*, the *New York Review of Books*, and *Commentary*.

Upon learning of Eichmann's arrest, she wrote to William Shawn, editor of the *New Yorker*, asking to cover the trial for the magazine:

> I feel that I have a personal obligation to be present at the Eichmann trial, both as a German-Jewish refugee and as a political philosopher. I believe that this trial is a unique opportunity to examine the nature of evil and the role of bureaucracy in the Holocaust. I am convinced that the Eichmann trial will be one of the most important events of our time, and I am determined to cover it in the most thoughtful and responsible way possible.[2]

He agreed, and what followed would be a critical moment in the history of Israel and the postwar era and in Arendt's career. "Eichmann in Jerusalem," the first of several articles (later collected as a book), was published in February 1963. Along with tremendous controversy, the articles birthed the phrase that is today most associated with Arendt: "the banality of evil."

This phrase is critical to both Arendt's project and this book. Most often, it is associated with the idea that ordinary people can be convinced to do terrible things. That's a compelling idea in and of itself, but it's not exactly what Arendt meant (and certainly wouldn't match her understanding of Eichmann).

To understand her argument, it's important to see how Eichmann surprised Arendt's expectations. In *The Origins of Totalitarianism*, borrowing from Kant, she described the appearance of "radical evil"[3] in the world. This evil, she said, can't be conceived in terms of Christian theology or the philosophical tradition of the West:

> We actually have nothing to fall back on in order to understand a phenomenon that nevertheless confronts us with its overpowering reality and breaks down all standards we know. There is only one thing that seems to be discernible: we may say that radical evil has emerged in connection with a system in which all men have become equally superfluous.[4]

For Kant, radical evil could appear when an evil premise—such as the idea that lying is okay if it's in my best interest—was carried out to its logical conclusions. In *Origins*, Arendt described how totalitarianism turned men and women "superfluous," erasing individual qualities and features and making each member of society a functionary, easily replaced by anyone else. The Nazi death camps were a kind of lab for this thesis, testing the bounds of the total destruction of an individual not only in the prisoners but also in the *Sonderkommando*—the higher-ranked prisoners—who oversaw them and the SS officers who ran the camps.

For Arendt, circa 1950, this explained the Holocaust. How else do you account for the sheer scale of industrialized murder, the inhumanity and indignity inflicted on millions of souls not just by a few evil leaders at the top of a regime but also by the citizens and soldiers who participated?

Arendt attended the Eichmann trial expecting to find an architect of radical evil. Indeed, the political leadership of the state of Israel and the leaders of the prosecution promised something along those lines, intending to hang the crimes of history against the Jewish people around his neck.

One can understand the desire to make the trial an inflection point in Israel's history. Eichmann would be the first Nazi criminal tried by the state, the others having been judged by an international court at Nuremberg. Thus, they brought the weight of the suffering of the Jewish people against him in the dock.

And yet, they didn't find a figure who could carry that weight. Eichmann was no monster, no Pharaoh, and no Haman.

It took Arendt some time to make sense of what she was observing. In a letter to a friend, she wrote, "Eichmann is actually stupid, but then somehow, he is not."[5] On one hand, he failed to live up to the monstrous expectations she (and much of the watching world) had anticipated; on the other hand, she couldn't find a reason to simply accept his tale of woe—that he was basically a good person who'd been caught up in the machinery of the Third Reich.

In time, she came to describe him as "terrifyingly normal,"[6] a bloviating and self-important careerist; a windbag who had never had an original thought in all of his life.

I think it's fair to say that Arendt found Eichmann personally repugnant and not simply for his Nazism. She found him repugnant as a mediocrity, a lifelong middle manager and social striver, ever eager to please the authorities. Eichmann was the sort of person who, when Mossad agents were prepping him to sneak him out of Argentina on a commercial flight, would remind them to dress him properly:

> The Nazi prisoner cooperated so fully that at one stage he reminded his captors that they had forgotten to put on his airline jacket. "That will arouse suspicion for I will be conspicuously different from the other members of the squad who are fully dressed," lectured Eichmann.[7]

For that reason, Arendt criticized those who tried to make something out of Eichmann that he decidedly wasn't. They "wanted to try the most abnormal monster the world had ever seen," she wrote of the prosecution. "They knew, of course, that it would have been very comforting indeed to believe that Eichmann was a monster"[8]—comforting because we could trace the horrors of the Holocaust to a suitable villain, not a bureaucrat.

But they never quite comprehended that the cliché-spouting middle manager in the dock in Jerusalem was precisely what he appeared to be. To be sure, Eichmann lied throughout the trial, minimizing his role and attempting to paint himself the victim of history. And yet it was precisely this version of Eichmann— the striving administrator—who had sent six million Jews to their death. He did so not acting as a stone-cold killer or mass murderer. Instead, he did it as one eager to impress his boss, inflate his importance to his peers, and contribute to the arc of history that was being ushered in by the Reich.

This presented a complexity for the prosecution and the judges, wrote Arendt:

> Foremost among the larger issues at stake in the Eichmann trial was the assumption current in all modern legal systems that intent to do wrong is necessary for the commission of a crime. On nothing, perhaps, has civilized jurisprudence prided itself more than on this taking into account of the subjective factor. Where this intent is absent, where for whatever reasons, even reasons of moral insanity, the ability to distinguish between right and wrong is impaired, we feel no crime has been committed.[9]

To borrow a phrase from the movie *The Dark Knight*: "Some men just want to watch the world burn,"[10] and they set it afire with clear-eyed awareness of where they stand in the moral universe. Surely that described some of the Nazis and many other criminals and sociopaths. But it didn't suit Eichmann. The preponderance of evidence pointed to something much worse:

> The trouble with Eichmann was precisely that so many were like him, and that the many were neither perverted nor sadistic, that they were, and still are, terribly and terrifyingly normal. From the viewpoint of our legal institutions and of our moral standards of judgment, this normality was much more terrifying than all the atrocities put together, for it implied—as had been said at Nuremberg over and over again by the defendants and their counsels—that this new type of criminal . . . commits his crimes under circumstances that make it well-nigh impossible for him to know or to feel that he is doing wrong.[11]

Eichmann was found guilty and sentenced to death. To Arendt, the sentence was problematic, not because Eichmann was innocent or deserved to live but because it failed to reckon with what he really was. Using these familiar categories, Eichmann was perplexing because he evidenced no "intent to do wrong" and no evidence of a guilty conscience; he was utterly convinced of the righteousness of his cause—even when he lied and tried to minimize his contributions to it.

Some have criticized Arendt for obscuring Eichmann's anti-Semitism. But as Arendt scholar Roger Berkowitz has argued, that misses the point. Arendt knew perfectly well that Eichmann was an anti-Semite, but she recognized that his anti-Semitism came from Nazi ideology—not the old-fashioned folk anti-Semitism of blood libel, or the czarist anti-Semitism in *The Protocols of the Elders of Zion*. Rather, as a Nazi loyalist, he believed in the "momentum of history" and the redemption of the "fatherland" and painted Jews as an obstacle in the march of progress.[12]

The closest the courts in Nuremberg had come to proving a guilty conscience among the Nazis was noting that they had scrambled to destroy documents outlining the Final Solution. But, Arendt writes, the Nuremberg trials

> proved no more than recognition that the law of mass murder, because of its novelty, was not yet accepted by other nations; or, in the language of the Nazis, that they had lost their fight to "liberate" mankind from the "rule of subhumans," especially from the domination of the Elders of Zion; or, in ordinary language, it proved no more than the admission of defeat. Would any one of them have suffered from a guilty conscience if they had won?[13]

In this, we can start to see the meaning of the banality of evil. It is not enough to simply say that ordinary men and women can do terrible things. Rather, it's that these terrible things are actually transformed in the moral universe of the Nazis into a *positive good*. The wholesale murder of an entire race was an act of liberation, and as such, murder became part of the state's everyday operations. Eichmann hadn't been recruited to Nazism because of his murderous instincts but rather because of his rootlessness, mediocrity, and lack of purpose.

Arendt was determined to present him to her readers as he appeared. As Berkowitz describes:

> Eichmann's motivations seemed to [Arendt] to be grounded in typical bourgeois drives. He was ambitious. He sought the recognition that came from success and the affirmation that flowed from belonging to a movement. He was, she concluded, not a monster, not stupid, but thoughtless. And it was this "absence of thinking—which is so ordinary an experience in our everyday life, where we have hardly the time, let alone the inclination, to stop and think"—that Arendt came to see as the dangerous wellspring of evil in modern times.[14]

Berkowitz acknowledges, along with some of Arendt's critics, that she "overstates her case." Eichmann "was not a mere

vacuum salesman who became a Nazi." Rather, he was someone who was thoroughly committed to the Nazi movement.
"Over and over," Berkowitz writes, "he expressed his courageous
willingness to die for his beliefs. He saw himself as a warrior,
someone who was willing to sacrifice his human feelings for the
greater importance of victory of the German Reich. He acted
out of a strong and unwavering commitment to Nazis and a
belief in victory."[15]

But Arendt was aware of all of this, Berkowitz says, and nonetheless concluded that Eichmann's evil was shallow and banal.
This was evident most clearly in his "almost total inability ever
to look at anything from the other fellow's point of view"[16]—
that is, an inability to *think*.

Arendt points to Eichmann's work in Vienna as evidence,
where he was the head of the Center for Jewish Emigration.
This was after the Anschluss—when Germany assumed control over Austria—and before the Final Solution. His job was
to arrange for the exit and deportation of as many Jews as
possible. This amounted to the wholesale extortion of forty-
five thousand Jews who were forced to pay exorbitant sums
for exit papers for themselves and loved ones while the Nazis
seized their property. And yet, from his perspective, Arendt
writes:

> He and his men and the Jews were all "pulling together." . . .
> The Jews "desired" to emigrate, and he, Eichmann, was there
> to help them, because it so happened that at the same time
> the Nazi authorities had expressed a desire to see their Reich
> *judenrein* ["cleansed of Jews"]. The two desires coincided, and
> he, Eichmann, could "do justice to both parties." At the trial,
> he never gave an inch when it came to this part of the story,
> although he agreed that today, when "times have changed so
> much," the Jews might not be too happy to recall this "pulling
> together" and he did not want "to hurt their feelings."[17]

She calls the taped confessions of this affair "a veritable goldmine for a psychologist—provided he is wise enough to understand that the horrible can be not only ludicrous but outright funny."[18] These exposed his hopeless inability to think. She writes:

> He was genuinely incapable of uttering a single sentence that was not a cliché. . . . To be sure, the judges were right when they finally told the accused that all he had said was "empty talk"—except that they thought the emptiness was feigned, and that the accused wished to cover up other thoughts which, though hideous, were not empty. This supposition seems refuted by the striking consistency with which Eichmann, despite his rather bad memory, repeated word for word the same stock phrases and self-invented clichés (when he did succeed in constructing a sentence of his own, he repeated it until it became a cliché) each time he referred to an incident or event of importance to him.[19]

This is one of the most important concepts in *Eichmann in Jerusalem*. Eichmann's inability to *speak* outside of clichés reflected his inability to think outside himself. "The longer one listened to him," she wrote, "the more obvious it became that his inability to speak was closely connected with an inability to think . . . from the standpoint of somebody else."[20]

Arendt understood fully that Eichmann was a liar. Her point was that his lying wasn't what made him impossible to communicate with; it was his total lack of thought, imagination, and empathy. Thus, to him, the Austrian Jews *wanted* to emigrate and were partners in his project, not the subjects of the violent disruption of their lives. As Berkowitz puts it, Eichmann's failure to think was a failure of imagination:

> It was his incapacity to see from the perspective of others the insanity of his ideological convictions that Arendt called his inability to think. It is this thoughtlessness, Arendt argues, that

117

allowed Eichmann and people like him to carry out one of the greatest crimes in history.[21]

It is fair (and perhaps necessary) to ask how it's possible to be both a committed ideologue and thoughtless. Critics of Arendt have pointed to this as a contradiction of terms, asserting that one cannot be both a true believer and "thoughtless." But this critique misunderstands the nature of totalitarian ideology, which is inherently reductive—the incessant conclusion of "one damned thing after another" based on a simplistic key to history. The allure of an ideology is that it flattens the complexity of the real world and thus insulates and inoculates a person from the need to think.

Marx—the father of all political ideologies—criticized religion as an "opiate for the masses." But as Arendt rightly pointed out, religion—especially religious fundamentalism—is anything but an opiate, because it sets the conscience on a knife's edge, making a person anxiously attuned to the state of their soul. Rather, *ideology* functions as an opiate in an age of rootlessness. Where the Enlightenment has turned all of our institutional bonds into anxiety-producing questions—Who will I love? What do I believe? What am I to do with my life?—ideology obliterates them entirely. Ideology eclipses these kinds of questions with the energy, noise, and momentum of a movement that can catch a person up and carry them along in a purpose-filled story. In this sense, it does not replace our fragile roots but simply numbs us from the ache of uncertainty created by them.

For Eichmann, the movement of Nazism provided a story in which he could find some measure of meaning and some aspirations toward greatness. He knew his limits as a mere bureaucrat—and yet in the Reich he could use those limited talents to usher in "history."

For the Nazis to succeed at the scale and breadth they did, they needed to enlist the help of the "terrifyingly normal" rank and file of German society. This is different from the suggestion that good people can be convinced to do bad things, or that the bureaucracy, rhetoric, and social conditioning of totalitarianism can simply bypass a person's moral compass. In the end, Arendt maintains that Eichmann is responsible for his actions and worthy of a death sentence. Yet she helps us see that the desire for belonging and purpose can make one susceptible to ideological evil.

Eichmann was captivated by the story of an ascendent Reich and the opportunity to discover purpose and meaning in its ends. Once he devoted himself to that story and purpose, he never questioned it, believing that the ends justified the means—whether that meant the deportation of Jews from Vienna or the transport of Jews from ghettos across Europe to the death camps.

Years later, in the preface for her unfinished work *The Life of the Mind*, Arendt reflected on her encounter with Eichmann and how it set the course for that work—connecting thinking and morality:

> I was struck by the manifest shallowness in the doer that made it impossible to trace the uncontestable evil of his deeds to any deeper level of roots or motives. The deeds were monstrous, but the doer—at least the very effective one now on trial—was quite ordinary, commonplace, and neither demonic nor monstrous. . . . Might the problem of good and evil, our faculty of telling right from wrong, be connected with our faculty of thought? . . . Could the activity of thinking as such, the habit of examining whatever happens to come to pass or to attract attention, regardless of results and specific content, could this activity be among the conditions that make men abstain from evildoing or even actually "condition" them against it?[22]

In this, her work came full circle. In discovering the banality of evil—the thoughtlessness of it—she made sense of the "ideal totalitarian subject" she'd described in *The Origins of*

Totalitarianism. That person had suspended any concern for the difference between truth and falsehood and accepted the iron logic of ideology as its substitute. Her diagnosis of Eichmann also reaffirmed the thesis of *The Human Condition*—that we must "think what we are doing."

In spite of the many ways that modernity had overemphasized the rational, the problem wasn't too much thinking; it was not enough.

Arendt after Eichmann

Arendt's encounter with Eichmann was life-altering. She was stunned by his inability to think, and it forced her to rethink and ultimately discard the notion of "radical evil." Evil, she would come to say later, can never be radical because it has no substance. It can be *horrible*, for certain—she of all people knew that was true. But it had no depth, no meaning; it is an emptiness that can only consume. And that emptiness was the very thing that makes evil capable of manifesting through mediocrities like Eichmann. As Amos Elon describes it:

> In *Eichmann in Jerusalem*, and in the bitter controversies about it that followed, she insisted that only good had any depth. Good can be radical; evil can never be radical, it can only be extreme, for it possesses neither depth nor any demonic dimension yet—and this is its horror!—it can spread like a fungus over the surface of the earth and lay waste the entire world. Evil comes from a failure to think. It defies thought for as soon as thought tries to engage itself with evil and examine the premises and principles from which it originates, it is frustrated because it finds nothing there. That is the banality of evil.[23]

Elon likens Arendt's conception of evil to the devil in Dostoyevsky's *The Brothers Karamazov*, who turns out to be a "shabby, stupid lout."[24] It's actually a theory of evil that's resonant with Christian teaching, where idolatry is the worship of hollow and dead idols, and where rebellion, chaos, and hell itself arise from humans rejecting goodness and God. Yes, evil can manifest in ways that are direct and terrifying, and it can be advanced by passion and hate, but it doesn't need them; it does just as well with a careerist like Eichmann. In fact, it *needs* figures like Eichmann to advance its purposes with the patina of normalcy.

This description was one of several topics of controversy that followed the publication of *Eichmann in Jerusalem*. As indicated above, many critics couldn't let go of the cartoonish picture of Eichmann as a bloodthirsty monster and thought Arendt downplayed his anti-Semitism. But even that controversy paled in comparison to the criticism that emerged over her comments about the *Judenräte*—Jewish civic leaders—during the Holocaust. These were the local council leaders and community elders who negotiated with Nazi authorities over issues like deportation schedules and conditions in the ghettos.

Perhaps the most notorious passage of all was this one:

Wherever Jews lived, there were recognized Jewish leaders, and this leadership, almost without exception, cooperated in one way or another, for one reason or another, with the Nazis. The whole truth was that if the Jewish people had really been unorganized and leaderless, there would have been chaos and plenty of misery but the total number of victims would hardly have been between four and a half and six million people.[25]

Arendt's arguments weren't entirely new. Raul Hilberg's *The Destruction of the European Jews*, published two years earlier, had made similar arguments about the efforts of Jewish councils and local leaders to minimize suffering by cooperating with Nazi authorities. In some ways, both Arendt and Hilberg pale in comparison to Tadeusz Borowski's descriptions in *This Way to the Gas, Ladies and Gentlemen*, published in 1951. Together, they represent a consensus that has largely been vindicated by history—that civic leaders were at best naive in their interactions with Nazis and at worst guilty of organizing the extermination of others in hopes of saving their own necks. These hopes, almost to a person, proved futile. One can imagine, though, that if you were skeptical of Arendt's portrayal of Eichmann as a mediocrity and not a monster, this description of Jewish councils added insult to injury.

That, indeed, was how many readers reacted—including some of Arendt's dearest friends and allies. She had, in their view, betrayed her people, blaming them for their own suffering while exonerating Eichmann for being too stupid to see through Nazi ideology. And while both of these accusations chase Arendt to this day, neither is accurate. We've already discussed her more complicated views of Eichmann (and will return to him momentarily), and there was the matter of her tone of voice in the original articles—as published in the *New Yorker*—which was often both biting and ironic.[26] She told the journalist Günter Gaus:

> That the tone of voice is predominantly ironic is completely true. . . . If people think that one can only write about these things in a solemn tone of voice. . . . Look, there are people who take it amiss—and I can understand that in a sense—that, for instance, I can still laugh. But I was really of the opinion that Eichmann was a buffoon.[27]

On the charge that she blamed the Jews for their suffering, she told Gaus:

> Nowhere in my book did I reproach the Jewish people with nonresistance. Someone else did that in the Eichmann trial, namely Mr. Hausner of the Israeli public prosecutor's office. I called such questions directed to the witnesses in Jerusalem both foolish and cruel.[28]

Her critique was not that they should have fought back or resisted (indeed, there were notable examples of those who did). She simply stated the fact that in hindsight, one could see that the strategies of these leaders didn't make things easier on the Jews; they made them easier on the Nazis, made their machinery of death operate with much greater efficiency.

To be a moral actor in dark times, then, one doesn't need superior intellect or superhuman strength; one simply needs to protect their capacity to *think*. This means resisting the seductive logic of ideology, being skeptical of a movement's meaning-making stories, and above all rejecting the idea that the consensus of others should compel us to suspend our capacity to judge.

Ideology and the Trial of Paul Petry

In chapter 1, I asked how it was that twenty-three men could, in one accord, make a judgment that would violate their own consciences. How could they make a judgment of Paul Petry that contradicted their knowledge of the *facts* and their sense of right and wrong?

Some people say that these men were sadists who loved power and authority enough to relish its abuse or who belonged to a celebrity cult that would unquestioningly do the bidding of their idol, Mark Driscoll. But neither of these explanations have ever struck me as sufficient. The unanimity of the verdict made sadism an unlikely explanation (how likely is it that all twenty-three shared such a pathology?). And as much as there might have been a cult of celebrity around Driscoll, celebrity worship doesn't strike me as the best motivator for abusive behavior. It lacks compulsive power—the ability to overcome a person's conscience.

Those explanations pale in comparison to the compulsive power of an ideological movement. Those at Mars Hill had a sense of belonging and a purpose that were powerful enough to distort their entire moral framework. As Arendt put it, part of the distorting effect of ideology is to invert temptation. Where the ordinary order of the world would have us intuit that lying is wrong, and one is tempted to push against that order when it suits their interests, ideology can invert the temptation. When an ideological end is in view—Driscoll's specific vision of advancing the mission of God—the temptation is that one can choose to do the *right* thing—voting against the elders of Mars Hill and standing by Petry.

This does not excuse those men, of course. It merely accounts for the distorted nature of their temptations, as does the oft-cited experience of Mars Hill members that, had they stood with Paul, they too would have lost everything.

Arendt's friend Mary McCarthy likened this experience to being told at gunpoint, "Kill your friend or I will kill you." A person who does this to you isn't forcing you to do anything, McCarthy said, but is merely tempting you. "And while a temptation where one's life is at stake may be a legal excuse for a crime," Arendt wrote, "it certainly is not a moral justification."[29]

The temptation each Mars Hill elder faced was to either fire and excommunicate Paul—knowing it was wrong—or face the same consequences for himself and his family. Taken on its merits, the story doesn't add up, for who could live with themselves knowing that they socially and spiritually "shot" their friend and then went about their business *as a pastor* like nothing had ever happened? The missing piece is the ideology—the promise that on the other side of this evil thing one must do, a glorious story and glorious future was being ushered in.

Seen this way, one can think of Driscoll and his team as the chief propagandists of Mars Hill: storytellers who were constantly articulating their distorted moral vision in order to keep their self-enclosed world intact. In the Third Reich, the propagandists explained to the masses that true bravery, true love of country meant the capacity to do terrible things. Similarly, D. T. Suzuki, the Zen Buddhism teacher of the twentieth century, distorted Buddhism into ideology during the Second World War. He was captivated by the grandiosity of the Japanese emperor and saw his militaristic ambitions as part of a grander cultural vision that could bring about utopian ends. Thus the war, with its bloody and annihilationist means, needed to be framed within the bounds of his religion. Suzuki writes:

> The uplifted sword has no will of its own, it is all of emptiness. It is like a flash of lightning. The man who is about to be struck down is also of emptiness, and so is the one who wields the sword. None of them are possessed of a mind that has any substantiality. As each of them is of emptiness and has no "mind" [*kokoro*], the striking man is not a man, the sword in his hands is not a sword, and the "I" who is about to be struck down is like the splitting of the spring breeze in a flash of lightning.[30]

The warrior, well-trained in Zen Buddhism, carries out his duty in an egoless state, not killing for his own sake but for universal principles—for the ideology. And "without a sense of an ego, there is no moral responsibility."[31] Indeed, even the victim does not suffer at the hands of the soldier. Rather, each person is simply playing their part in enacting the course of history. The soldier has "no desire to harm anybody" while the enemy "appears and makes himself a victim."[32]

In other words, a soldier on the battlefield or one committing atrocities in the name of the emperor was not killing his fellow human beings, be they man, woman, or child; he was releasing them from the illusions of their reality.

I include the example of Suzuki here because it perfectly illustrates the old cliché that "the heart wants what the heart wants." Ideology has a hypnotic and persuasive power on the spiritual imagination regardless of a person's context. Often, the crisis we see unfolding in the church is blamed on a certain ecclesiastical tradition or an underlying theology about gender, sexuality, the nature of the Scriptures, or the model of church governance. But the fact is that while some beliefs might be more easily recruited for purposes of abuse, any belief—regardless of tradition or religion—can be flattened into an ideology and used to justify horrors.

The power of the ideology isn't in the details of doctrine or dogma; it's in the power of the stories being told and the overarching promise—the glorious future of the new reich, the empire, or in our case, the church that's going to change the world.

My point is not to equivocate between the evil of the Axis powers and the evil that was manifest at Mars Hill. There is such a thing as scale and gravity of impact, and the gap between the damage done by the great evil powers of the twentieth century and that of abusive evangelical churches is almost immeasurable.

But it's critical to see that they share an architecture. The allure of a simple explanation for what ails us—the lack of real men or of real leadership, for example—combined with the promise of a utopian future and a church that will "change the world," can motivate terrible actions and has done so throughout our recent history.

Who Am I to Judge?

There is a point at which everyone has their own Pontius Pilate moment and decides—even against their own conscience—"Who am I to judge?" The result isn't that they wash their hands of dirty business and go to bed; like Pilate, they too have a part to play. When faced with the temptation of standing with someone like Paul Petry, they lend their voice to the arguments against him, they cast their votes, they push against dissenters, and then they go back to their work "for the sake of the mission."

The great temptation for anyone living in the modern age—whether we're talking about evangelicals, politicians, or academics—is to find a grandiose story and a grandiose leader to give ourselves away to. We want the opiate-like effect that obliterates the anxieties of identity, and we want to feel like we're part of something that matters and lasts.

To resist that means accepting the incomprehensibility of much of life. It means insisting on the tragic aspects of the world. It means facing our anxieties on their own terms and building an identity with the brittle tools available to us. It probably means investing in institutions and accepting that we may not find what we're looking for in our lifetime. Most of all, it means maintaining our capacity to think and judge.

And with that in mind, we can begin to talk about resistance.

PART 2

RESISTING DARK TIMES

6

Eugene Peterson, Charlie Brown, and Resistance in Dark Times

What is resistance in dark times?

For those who wish to see a better and more beautiful church, the great temptation comes in the form of another movement— one promising reform with yet another key to history. These exist already. Some gather around personalities who fashion themselves as modern Martin Luthers—celebrities waging war against Celebrity—and some organize around post-evangelical theologies that would lose the gospel in the efforts to save it.

But these efforts tend to be reductionistic; that is how they give away their ideological tendencies. Simple cures to complex problems are almost always snake oil.

What the church needs is to practice anti-ideology. It needs to reject the premises of comprehensibility and certainty and display a healthy skepticism of "world-changing" ambition. This posture resists cynicism on one hand, believing that there is always reason to hope, and resists grandiosity on the other, believing that we are always at the mercy of God, uncertainty, and complexity.

Resisting evangelical ideologies in all their forms isn't going to look like light in the darkness. Rather, it will be something quieter, something unimpressive, a "mere" church that seeks to do those things that redeemed people do—praying, discipling, celebrating, grieving, and sharing one another's burdens. It doesn't mean that the Christian life has to be primarily austere or ascetic, and it doesn't mean that church will be dull, music will be old, and congregations will be small. But it does mean that the ways we measure "success" will change.

Thankfully, we are not without examples.

A Seattle Pilgrimage

In April 2022, I visited Seattle for the first time in about a decade. I'd recorded all of *The Rise and Fall of Mars Hill* from a distance, largely because of travel limitations and uncertainties related to the COVID-19 pandemic. The main episodes of the series were completed, and I was visiting a handful of people who'd contributed to the series to talk about the show, thank them, and record a few conversations.

On my first day there, I drove around the city with former members of Mars Hill, visiting the old facilities, walking through the "living history" of the place, and getting impromptu lessons on the history of Seattle. It's one of the things that I loved most about working on the series—getting to vicariously enjoy the affection these former pastors and members had for the city itself.

Ballard was the center of most of my meetings and was really the center of the Mars story. The Leary Way building was where I'd come to really know Mars Hill years earlier when I had visited the church for conferences and events. It was where the church experienced its most explosive growth, where Driscoll preached his most memorable (for good or ill) sermons, and where the church's influence on the Young, Restless, and Reformed movement had been at its peak.

Ballard used to be what Robert Capon might have called "a real place," rooted in a people and a history—births, marriages, deaths, burials, little triumphs and tragedies that unfolded in the tightly packed rows of houses surrounding warehouses, processing plants, and industrial buildings. Today, it's surging with renovations and new construction. A tall building full of shops and condominiums sits next to the old Leary Way building, complete with a Ross Dress for Less and a gourmet doughnut shop. Following the life cycles of many cities, the particularities of Ballard's past have been squeezed out by generic chain stores.

"This was all Scandinavians when it was built," former Mars Hill pastor Tim Smith told me as we drove past rows of hundred-year-old houses packed in between rows of warehouses. "They were fishermen before they moved to the states and rode trains out West, and they set this up as a big industrial fishing neighborhood." When the Smiths and other Mars Hill families came here, he said, there were a lot of family-owned small businesses and many second- and third-generation Danish and Norwegian residents.

In a funny way, the transformation of Ballard echoes that of Mars Hill. The church had grown out of the soil of Seattle, infused with its music, language, aesthetics, and mood. Over time, as it took on the character of a movement with global ambitions, the fingerprints of the city disappeared in order to make it more appealing to the masses. That flattening of the church's identity was an inevitable result of its ideology. As Mars Hill Global, its leaders wanted to "reach the city" and "change the world," and the tools that enable one to do that are all codified by mass culture—mass marketing, mass entertainment, mass media.

For a movement, that means treating individuals as mass persons and variables in an equation, an "anyone" who is actually no one. Movements require seeing people as mere members of a group whose primary contribution is to add to the movement's momentum and energy. They're encouraged to find a sense of who they are in what they can do for the movement, and they'll increasingly conform to the movement's values—actively erasing their own personal desires and preferences such that they embody another's. Those who loved the city, and who loved Mars Hill as part of the city, were the ones whose hearts were broken first.

"We're still here, dude," said one former member. "We're all still here." We were standing in the lobby of his offices, just a few blocks away from the Leary Way building. He rattled off the nearby addresses of half a dozen people from the church as well as a few choice words about those who left. The art on his office walls told Seattle's stories—bands, entrepreneurs, brands, photos of the city's landscape. "We cared about Seattle," he said.

The visit left me feeling haunted and full of melancholy. On one hand, there are strange graces in the shadow of Mars Hill—the friendships and marriages that weathered the storms, the faith that endures in new and surprising ways. But on the other hand, there is also this palpable absence. For many, Mars Hill was the most intensely meaningful experience of their lives—but there are bad reasons for that intensity.

There's also a broader sadness that accompanies the Mars Hill story—one that I carried before I ever began thinking about making a podcast. It came from my own story, my own sense of being caught up in a mission to change the world, and my own collision with reality when the rootlessness of my "movement" led to disillusionment.

I drove to the Airbnb my executive producer and I had rented in the Queen Anne neighborhood. I had a few hours to kill before dinner and decided to sit on the porch and enjoy the rare Seattle sunshine with a book I'd been meaning to open for a long time: Winn Collier's biography of Eugene Peterson, *A Burning in My Bones.*

Peterson is probably best known as the translator of The Message, the Bible paraphrase that began as a pastoral project and became a bestseller. He was an iconoclast in the age of the celebrity pastor. He devoted thirty-nine years of ministry to one congregation, where he was committed to never letting the church grow so large that he couldn't remember every member's name. Along with his translations, he wrote dozens of books, including works of pastoral theology that are at once countercultural, prophetic, and grace-filled. Needless to say, I am a fan.

And at that particular moment, I was looking forward to spending some time in his presence, or rather, in the presence of his memory (he died in 2018). I wanted to hear the story of a pastor who'd resisted the trappings and temptations that led so many others to wreak havoc in countless congregations.

Along with immersing myself in the Mars Hill story, I'd spent two years flooded with stories from Christians who'd experienced similar tragedies in other churches. It was a strange, sacred stewardship, and yet the gravity of it could tempt a person to despair. I knew enough about Peterson's life and legacy to believe this book would be a breath of fresh air.

I flipped it open and began reading Peterson's story. In pretty short order, I found myself at the beginning of chapter 3, reading about Herman and Matilda Peterson—Eugene's Swedish grandparents.

With the promise of jobs, the support of the Scandinavian community gathered around the Ballard neighborhood of Seattle, Washington, and a longing for a familiar expanse of ocean, they put down roots. In 1923, the Ballard Norwegians founded

Fremont Tabernacle, an Assemblies of God church in East Stan-
wood, Washington, where the Petersons had moved.[1]

It's a little thing, I know. Just a strange, happy coincidence.
But it leapt off the page at me in that moment like the voice
of Gabriel.

I'd spent the day immersed in stories that stirred a nostalgic
affection for Seattle in general and for Ballard and its residents
in particular. And yet, at the end of that day, the overwhelming
feeling was one of loss and lament. Not because I wished Mars
Hill still stood there, but because I wished that the ties that
bonded that community together hadn't been severed. I wished
that the church could *matter* without becoming all-consuming.
I wished ideology hadn't corrupted the gospel message, and I
wished the wounds that so many had so vulnerably shared had
never been caused—especially because they'd been caused by
pastors and church leaders.

So when I saw the shadow of Peterson pass through the
streets of Ballard, if only from a distance, it took my breath
away. The contrast was not simply between Driscoll and Peterson but between their ways of seeing the world, the church,
and the gospel, and the entire movement-driven ethos of the
megachurch phenomenon.

When I was in ministry, serving at a church that was counted
among America's "fastest growing churches," I scoffed at Peterson's commitment to pastoring a small church. Who was he
to put a limit on the work of the Spirit? To stopper the spread
of the gospel? What arrogance, I thought. Or—and this is even
worse—maybe he just didn't have what it took to grow a bigger
church. Maybe his gifts were best expressed on the page and
not in the pulpit, and that's why the church never got "too big"
for his liking.

What I realize now is that Peterson's commitment was actually to keep the church a "place." It was about preserving the

stories, texture, and weirdness of a given community. Had he planted in Ballard, he'd have never lost that gray Seattle ethos or the weather-beaten sense of belonging. Peterson pastored people—real people, not mass people, not abstractions.

Collier describes the formation of that sensibility just a few pages after mentioning Ballard in the book. Young Eugene had grown up hearing romanticized stories about his uncle Sven— his mom's charming brother. Only years later did Eugene learn that Sven was abusive toward his wife. When he, drunk and broke, tried to force her out to walk the streets and sell herself, she pulled his own gun on him and killed him.

Peterson himself wrote that Sven "inoculated me against 'one answer' systems of spiritual care." He writes:

> Thanks to Sven, I was being prepared to understand a congregation as a gathering of people that requires a context as large as the Bible itself if we are to deal with the ambiguities of life in the actual circumstances in which people live them. . . . For me, my congregation would become a work-in-progress—a novel in which everyone and everything is connected in a salvation story in which Jesus has the last word. No reductions to stereotype.[2]

I'm not sure I could articulate a better way to approach the world that was designed to contrast with ideology's simplicity and iron logic. Peterson can look at Sven and explode outward a universe full of complexity and contradiction, and while doing so can be incredibly perplexing, it isn't distorting. That's because it relies, at its roots, on the conviction that the world is not something that can be reduced and comprehended—only beheld.

A posture of beholding rather than manipulating restrains us in healthy ways. Not only does this posture caution us against grandiose, world-changing ambitions; it also keeps us open to the work of God. The pastor's job is not to "cast a vision" for a spiritual factory in which every Sven can become an idealized Christian. Instead, they are to attend to every member in the presence of God, looking for evidence that he is at work. As Peterson puts it:

> The assumption of spirituality is that always God is doing something before I know it. So the task is not to get God to do something I think needs to be done, but to become aware of what God is doing so that I can respond to it and participate and take delight in it.[3]

This posture is anti-ideology. It is rooted in a humbled sense that God is at work in incomprehensible ways. It doesn't invite strategic planning; it invites prayer and humility. It doesn't require "visionary leadership," but it does require "eyes to see"— the ability to attend to the work of God in the lives of his people. Such a pastor won't be seduced by ideology and won't be tempted to craft their own; the dizzying complexity of each person God puts before them will scare that desire right out of them.

Repentance as Rest

One of Peterson's translations from the book of Isaiah has haunted me. I first encountered the passage out of context, applied to the spiritual disciplines. Isaiah 30:15 says, "In returning and rest you shall be saved; in quietness and in trust shall be your strength" (ESV).

The book I was reading used this verse as a proof text for the need for solitude and silence, and that application isn't entirely off base. Israel is eagerly searching for an answer to their suffering—specifically, to their persecution. Isaiah's point is that God is their strength, and God will provide their redemption. But the passage takes on a different tone when you read the next phrase: "But you were unwilling" (v. 15 ESV).

Without that phrase, the passage reads like kitchen art one might buy at Hobby Lobby. But Isaiah's point was to lay bare something about the human heart. Here's how Peterson translates the passage (and the larger context):

> God, the Master, The Holy of Israel,
>   has this solemn counsel:
> "Your salvation requires you to turn back to me
>   and stop your silly efforts to save yourselves.
> Your strength will come from settling down
>   in complete dependence on me—
> The very thing
>   you've been unwilling to do. . . .
> There'll be nothing left of you—
>   a flagpole on a hill with no flag,
>   a signpost on a roadside with the sign torn off." (vv.
>   15–17 The Message)

Peterson's translation helps us see that this passage is about the temptations of power. God made Israel unique among the nations as his covenant community, and he invites them to rest in him in order to experience redemption. Doing so is an act of trust, relinquishing any claims on control of the outcome of our circumstances.

At the time of Isaiah's writing, Israel was divided. The Northern Kingdom had already fallen under the rule of the Assyrians, and the Southern Kingdom was feeling pressured. They were tempted to seek help from their Egyptian neighbors rather than trust in God to deliver them.

Many modern evangelicals, living in the milieu of secularism, disenchantment, polarization, and extremism, sense that their faith is under siege. God invites his church to find its strength by settling down "in complete dependence on me" rather than reaching for the tools of modernity—ideology, celebrity, and movements.

Peterson translates:

> You've said, "No way! We'll rush off on horseback!"
> You'll rush off, all right! Just not far enough! (The
> Message)

Here, the Southern Kingdom of Israel is looking to horses from Egypt for their strength and protection. A modern analog would be trusting in a neighboring nation's military power—their tanks or fighter planes. The point is that the kingdom believes it has nothing to fear because it has recruited these powers—both political and symbolic—to insulate it from its enemies.

And the modern evangelical movement has its own horses. In recent history, those horses have included figures like Mark Driscoll and Bill Hybels and the movements they led. But there have been many others. It's hard not to think about the 1980s when national politics was cast as a cosmic battle between good and evil. Charismatic figures such as Lauren Stratford and Mike Warnke regaled evangelicals with stories of satanic cabals that were butchering children and pulling the levers in places of global power. Judge Paul Pressler and Paige Patterson were leading a "conservative resurgence" inside the Southern Baptist Convention, overhauling the denomination's institutions and cleaning house of anyone who didn't meet their definition of orthodoxy. Bill Gothard was expanding his Institute in Basic Life Principles, casting a vision for a new way of educating children and resisting the liberalizing influences of public education and pop culture. Pat Robertson and Jerry Falwell gave us the Christian Coalition and Moral Majority, galvanizing white evangelical support for the Republican Party.

They were horses, all of them—powerful figures who were offering new ways to wage war against a secular society. And yet, when we assess the cumulative damage they've done to the church's witness, it's stunning. Driscoll and Hybels we've accounted for. Stratford and Warnke were hoaxers who made millions of dollars on fabricated stories and who stirred a moral panic that led to thousands of false accusations of satanic ritual abuse. Pressler was raging against the sexual revolution from platforms around the country while sexually assaulting young men and boys at his home. Patterson was removed from his leadership roles in 2018 for covering up sexual assault at his seminary. Gothard has been credibly accused of enabling abuse and grooming young girls. The hypocrisy of evangelicals demanding support for the GOP was exposed in 2016 when they aligned behind Donald Trump—who embodied all of the moral failings they'd pinned on their opposition for decades. And that's just to name a few. Each one came with grandiose, world-changing promises.

> You've said, "We'll ride off on fast horses!"

In the end, though, their achievements didn't outweigh the incredible damage of their shadows and sins. We didn't know it, but when we thought we were choosing the weapons that we'd go to war with, we were choosing the methods of our own destruction.

> You've said, "We'll ride off on fast horses!"
>   Do you think your pursuers ride old nags?
> Think again: A thousand of you will scatter before one
>   attacker. (The Message)

We wanted the power they offered. Forty years later, we've only begun to reckon with the damage they've done. Too many believers I know would find some resonance with Isaiah's image:

> There'll be nothing left of you—
>   a flagpole on a hill with no flag,

141

> a signpost on a roadside with the sign torn off. (The
> Message)

How many young people were kept at risk in the presence of predators because the church wanted to look the other way for powerful leaders like Pressler and Gothard? How many eager to serve the church had their faith shattered by abusive and narcissistic leaders? The political priorities of the Trump era haven't just driven evangelicals from the GOP; it's driven Christians away from evangelicalism.

And yet, we're still here—and I'd imagine if you're still reading this, you're wondering what a better way might look like. Even on the other side of error and devastation, Isaiah says that God hasn't abandoned his people, and he hasn't abandoned his plan to rebuild a broken world.

> But God's not finished. He's waiting around to be
> gracious to you.
> He's gathering strength to show mercy to you. (v. 18
> The Message)

There is an opportunity, amid the brokenness of this moment, for a different kind of witness; an opportunity for a church to emerge from the ashes that is built—that is *rebuilt*—by the grace and mercy that God has prepared for his people.

Peterson's images—the flagpole with no flag and the road sign with no sign—invoke a third image for me, one that illustrates the stark contrast between ambition and reality and that also illustrates the power of God's grace to transform "mere" circumstances into something beautiful. It's Charlie Brown's Christmas tree from *A Charlie Brown Christmas*.

This brilliant little television special, produced in 1965, captured the melancholy ethos of modern Christmas perfectly. Charlie Brown wants to feel like celebrating Christmas, but of course, he can't get in the spirit of things. When he's tasked with buying the Christmas tree, he chooses a frail, sickly tree with hardly a needle or branch. "I think it needs me,"[4] he says, and he's partially right.

But when he delivers the tree, it can hardly hold an ornament, and Charlie becomes the laughingstock. He loses it, asking what all the stress and chaos of Christmas is really for. His friend Linus offers an answer, dropping his security blanket and reciting the Gospel of Luke:

"Behold, I bring you good tidings of great joy, which shall be to all people. For unto you is born this day in the City of David a Savior, which is Christ the Lord. And this shall be a sign unto you; Ye shall find the babe wrapped in swaddling clothes, lying in a manger." And suddenly there was with the angel a multitude of the heavenly host praising God, and saying, "Glory to God in the highest, and on earth peace, good will toward men." (Luke 2:10–14 KJV)

Charlie, not yet convinced, leaves the room, and Linus turns to the sad little tree. "I never thought it was such a bad little tree. It's not bad at all, really. Maybe it just needs a little love." Together with the rest of the gang, they decorate the tree and—in its own little way—it bursts to life. They step back and begin to sing. Charlie returns, drawn by the music. When they spot him, they shout in unison, "Merry Christmas, Charlie Brown!"

It's an elegant story about the transformative power of love. Charlie Brown intuited that the tree needed love, but because he was looking inward, trying to gin up some Christmas spirit, he didn't have what the tree actually needed. Linus can name what the tree needs because he knows what Christmas is all about, and in loving Charlie Brown's tree, he and the other Peanuts characters are able to love Charlie Brown back into the gang, into the spirit of Christmas.

The tree is simply a stand-in for Charlie himself—a bedraggled, world-weary figure. His friends, however imperfect, are his little church. Together they embody the power of grace to cut through the loneliness and anxiety that mark life in the modern world. It comes when people, despite their differences, struggles, conflicts, and flaws, love one another unconditionally. The Peanuts gang have a way of telling that story throughout their comics and cartoons, but none did so more explicitly than this Christmas special.

I imagine the church in dark times being a bit like Charlie Brown's Christmas tree: world-weary, bedraggled, lacking the substance and strength to hold itself up. But even in such a condition, as an object of love, it has immense potential. Something beautiful can emerge from the ashes.

Practicing Resistance

In what follows, I'll describe some practices that I think are necessary for the church to resist dark times. The goal is not "big tent revival"—overflowing pews, lines of people to make confessions of faith and get baptized, thousands and thousands joining local churches. Perhaps that's in God's plan, and I'll be the first to celebrate it if it is. But I mean something much simpler than that. Perhaps the church can be revived like one revives a boxer who's been knocked unconscious. Not simply waking someone up but bringing their whole consciousness back to the real world after being stupefied.

The first practice is solitude, which is essential to thinking in any world—especially one so malformed by ideology, distraction, mass culture, and movements. With solitude, one discovers the foundation to not only a life of thought and a life of prayer but to all the practices of spiritual formation.

Next is storytelling and culture making. The great Russian dissident Aleksandr Solzhenitsyn took seriously Dostoyevsky's idea that "beauty will save the world," and in his own writing about the resilience of the human spirit and the unquenchable power of faith, he helped bring down a communist regime.[5] Likewise, Hannah Arendt devoted an enormous amount of her own life to the study of literature and poetry, believing that there was something about beauty that could preserve our humanity under oppression. I'll explore the necessity of making beautiful things and telling meaningful stories to break through to people in dark times.

Finally, I'll talk about worship. It may seem backward to put worship last—since even I would agree it's the foremost of these practices in order of importance. But what I will argue is that worship, in both the broad (all of life) sense and narrow (gathered with God's people) sense, is meant to be a gathering up of all we are and all we do in an offering of love to God. As people disoriented by dark times, it will serve us well to begin with these other, life-orienting practices in order to better understand what I'm talking about when I talk about worship.

I must say—when I consider these practices together, I'm genuinely optimistic. These aren't obligations imposed on God's people as a means to transform them like a pressure cooker; they are gifts of God for the people of God. They invite us into experiences driven by love and desire, and they promise encounters with the living God along the way.

So if you're tired and weary, if you feel like a stripped road sign, consider this an invitation to an encounter with the God who longs to be gracious to you—the God who knows that all you need is a little love.

7

Solitude and Thinking

In 1975, Hannah Arendt was given the Sonning Prize, a Danish culture prize for contributions made to European culture.

Arendt felt conflicted. On one hand, she was exceedingly well-mannered and didn't want to reject the prize out of some misguided sense that she was above it. On the other hand, she had reservations about accepting it. In the end, in a gesture that was so fitting with her nature, she accepted the prize but gave an acceptance speech that acknowledged both her personal reservations and her concerns about what such a prize might do to shape the nature and character of a thinking person.

It's a remarkable speech and is among my favorite things Arendt ever wrote. It is personal in ways that her writing often is not, and it boils down some fundamental convictions she held about what it meant to remain thoughtful—which is to say, *virtuous*—in dark times.

She began by acknowledging the irony of being honored for contributions to European culture as a citizen of the United States. That citizenship wasn't simply a result of circumstance, since after the war she might have returned to Germany or joined many of her friends and colleagues who emigrated to Israel. But she had "consciously" and "voluntarily" naturalized because she found America to have a "government of law and not of men."[1] This was in contrast to Europe, "with their homogeneous populations, their organic sense of history, their more or less decisive division into classes, and their national sovereignty with its notion of *raison d'état*."[2]

By contrast, in America she could enjoy "the freedom of becoming a citizen without having to pay the price of assimilation." This put her at odds not so much with her fellow citizens but with her fellow émigrés who "tried very hard to . . . behave, to sound, and to feel like 'true Americans.'" This never appealed to Arendt. "My trouble was that I had never wished to belong, not even in Germany."[3]

This is the experience of the pariah—the outsider who either won't or can't assimilate into a larger culture. She was born a pariah as a Jew in Germany, where she never quite belonged to the nation; as secular Jews, her family never quite belonged to the Jewish diaspora either. By the time she came to America, it was a status she treasured and protected, enabling her to see, hear, and think differently about the world around her.

This is in part what made her so uncomfortable about the prize: it offered a sense of acceptance in an intellectual milieu where she would have preferred to remain an outsider. Indeed, to ensure there was no doubt about her outsider status, she began her speech by mentioning the deeper irony of this recognition—that she "left Europe thirty-five years ago by no means voluntarily."[4] This continent, and her home nation in particular, had wished her dead, and her intellectual contributions were largely a body of work produced in response to those events.

A second reservation was related, but more personal. It had been fourteen years since she first encountered Eichmann and the banality of evil. Since then, she'd only become more convinced of the moral imperative of the capacity to think and judge, and one hedge that protected that capacity felt threatened by the Sonning Prize.

Elsewhere in the talk, she describes embracing "old Epicurus' exhortation to the philosopher . . . 'live in hiding.'"[5] That impulse, she says, is an essential practice for thinking in dark times, and the allure of recognition—including in a prestigious venue like this one—threatened the sanctity of that solitude. Arendt knew all too well of those who'd allowed themselves to become captive to the longing for recognition:

> There existed after World War I a curious social structure . . . which could best be described as an international "society of celebrities." . . . It is true that none of those "internationals" of the twenties responded very well to their collective expectation of solidarity in the thirties, but it is, I think, also irrefutable that no one of them crumbled faster or threw the rest into greater despair than the entire sudden collapse of this apolitical society whose members, spoilt by the "radiant power of fame," were less able to cope with catastrophe than the nonfamous multitudes who were only deprived of the protective power of their passports.[6]

With the phrase "society of celebrities," Arendt affixes two labels to this group, each one subject to a fair amount of contempt. With "celebrity," she indicates that they were skilled at making themselves "celebrated" by the media, as opposed to those who are known for accomplishing great deeds (the classic definition of fame). This phenomenon emerged in the nineteenth century with the rise of mass media and the emergence of those who had the savvy, instincts, and talents to manipulate them. This would be contemptible enough on its own, but she also calls them a "society," and close readers of Arendt will detect even more scorn in this word.

She writes about society in *The Human Condition*, her most explicit work of political philosophy. In it, she introduces "the social" as a third realm of human experience that exists somewhere between the public and private. For the Greeks and Romans, the public realm was the realm of politics—actions and speech meant to persuade and guide the decision-making bodies (senators and citizens). The private realm is the realm of everyday life, where our basic needs are met, religion is generally practiced or ignored, and family and household business take place. Arendt holds both to be essential; the public realm is where culture is made and transformed, and the private realm is where we experience moral formation, love, and friendship.[7]

To these classical categories Arendt introduces the social realm, which she says has its reference point in the "high society" that filled the courts of kings during the late medieval period. This inner circle of aristocrats and members of the royal family enjoyed power and privilege in terms of both their wealth and their proximity to the king. But their power had severe limits; it was always only an expression or extension of the king's. Were they ever to find themselves crosswise of him, they'd quickly discover those limits.

In contrast to the Greek *polis*, the only person who had freedom in the public realm under such an arrangement was the king. Everyone else's speech and rights were subject to his whims. With the rise of Western-style democracy came the expansion of the public realm, making it a place where citizens of all sorts could ascend. Along with that came the Industrial Revolution, which transformed economic conditions in a way that made it possible for far more people to have the free time necessary to partake in the public realm than in Greece or Rome.

That economic transformation also created instability among class divisions, making it possible for the poor to become wealthy and the wealthy to more easily become poor.

One of the trade-offs (according to Arendt) is that people are less concerned with the collective good of the state or nation and more concerned with their own prosperity. Not only are they wanting to achieve economic success; they also develop the habits and means of signaling that economic success—as well as the means of signaling a sense of belonging that connects them with important (or merely fashionable) ideas and groups. Charles Taylor calls that signaling "mutual display"[8]— the subtle means by which I indicate that I'm "in the know" and "part of the group": the car I drive, the place I send my kids to school, the clothes I buy, the food I eat.

The pressures to conform to these unwritten standards are immense. While human beings have always had ways of signaling who is "in" and "out" of any community, doing so through consumer choices and implicit codes of conduct is unique to the modern era. Taylor rightly links this tendency to the issues of identity we discussed earlier in this book. It also links to Arendt's notion of the social, since these acts and gestures are only meaningful as signals; they're powerless and empty as political acts. Such gestures—posts on social media, bumper stickers on our car, the purchase of Veblen goods—are entirely self-interested, resulting in personal benefit in the form of social standing or social capital. They indicate belonging.

The public realm is a place of political action, where individuals attempt to persuade and direct their fellow citizens. The only persuasion taking place in the social realm is an attempt to convince one's neighbors of your status. Actions in this realm are motivated entirely by economic and social self-interest.

The trouble is that the social realm consumes our attention in ways that rob us of both the public and private realms. On one hand, we perform what might otherwise be in the private realm—actions related to love, friendship, family, religion, and household—in such a way as to make them visible in the social realm. The social realm provides incentives to make this transition, rewarding us for being the type of person who performs this sort of loving behavior. On the other hand, because the social realm emphasizes our self-interests, it distorts and diminishes our interest in the public realm, where our collective interests are debated and decided and where the actors on the world stage bear responsibility for their actions.

It's a fascinating outcome, something that fits neatly in between Orwell's predictions of a future in which humanity was ruled by obsessive and intrusive overlords and Huxley's predictions of a humanity numbed into quiet submission through consumerism and pharmacology. No force was necessary to drive people out of the public sphere and away from the political, since their self-interests drove them into the social realm, where they indulged consumer and economic interests in a race to display their status. At the same time, the social realm has rigid codes—rigid though unwritten and ever-evolving—by which people must abide if they hope to maintain their status. These differ widely according to context; the social code of the Upper East Side of Manhattan is very different from that of Franklin, Tennessee, and both are very different from that of Calle Ocho in Miami. But a resident of each place could quickly identify the necessary signals, shibboleths, and sacred cows that define the ins and outs of their community.

So it was with the "society of celebrities." They occupied a celebrated place in the media after the First World War, and in no small part they succeeded because they carefully navigated the social realm they inhabited. They wanted to bask in the "radiant power of fame," less interested in fame and achievement itself and more interested in admission into the celebrated communities of the famous. As Arendt describes in *The Origins of Totalitarianism*, "Thus they became outstanding reviewers, critics, collectors, and organizers of what was famous."[9]

For this reason—their interest in social achievement rather than actual intellectual or artistic achievement—they were

spectacularly incapable of responding meaningfully to the ca-
tastrophe of the 1930s. They had mistaken their acceptance in
the social realm with acceptance in the public realm, which is
to say that they'd mistaken it for political acceptance. When
others were "deprived only of their passports," their illusions
of belonging in this broader world collapsed as well, and it
sent them into despair.

By 1975, when Arendt gave her speech, they were forgotten.
This wasn't simply because they'd perished in the Holocaust,
though some surely did. Rather, they had failed to find a space
for themselves in the world that was more permanent than
their social milieu. "Nothing is more transient in our world,
less stable and solid, than that form of success which brings
fame," Arendt said. "Nothing comes swifter and more readily
than oblivion."[10]

She tells this story because the occasion of the speech had
awakened her memories of them and stirred a kind of "crisis of
identity" in her. The fact that she'd resisted the pull of celebrity
wasn't just a practical, academic, or spiritual decision; it was
a survival mechanism. As a philosopher, a Jew, and a pariah,
she couldn't afford for the "radiant power of fame" to draw
her out of the private realm where her most meaningful work
actually took place.

And yet, there she stood, delivering this speech in Denmark.
To make peace with the recognition the award afforded, Arendt
invokes the idea of the "persona," in both its literal and its
metaphorical sense.

[In the original Latin] *persona* . . . referred to the actor's mask
that covered his individual "personal" face and indicated to
the spectator the role and the part of the actor in the play.
But in this mask, which was designed and determined by the
play, there existed a broad opening at the place of the mouth
through which the individual, undisguised voice of the actor

153

could sound. It is from this sounding through that the word *persona* was derived: *per-sonare*, "to sound through," is the verb of which *persona*, the mask, is the noun.[11]

To occupy the space in which she stood for this speech, she had to understand it as embodying a persona or wearing a mask, a momentary appearance as a role player for this moment of recognition.

> We always appear in a world which is a stage and are recognized according to the roles which our professions assign us, as physicians or lawyers, as authors or publishers, as teachers or students, and so on. . . . The advantage of adopting the notion of *persona* for my considerations lies in the fact that the masks or roles which the world assigns us, and which we must accept and even acquire if we wish to take part in the world's play at all, are exchangeable; . . . they are not a permanent fixture annexed to our inner self.[12]

Arendt is describing a private realm that is insulated from the seduction of the social. It requires us to remember that our appearances in the world, regardless of how significant or laudatory they may be, are merely that—appearances and not who we truly are. Keeping that distinction is essential if we're to maintain our consciences and morality.

We must always be aware that whatever energy and excitement we might experience in public, those experiences don't define us, and our appearances in public don't constitute the "real me." Whatever the "real me" is—my "authentic self" or "true self" as it's often called—doesn't appear in public at all and can hardly appear in its complex entirety even to myself.

Arendt ends her speech comforted by the knowledge that afterward, she will return to solitude and to the ambiguous sense of self that is free not to perform but to think.

It is in this sense that I can come to terms with appearing here as a "public figure" for the purpose of a public event. It means that when the events for which the mask was designed are over, and I have finished using and abusing my individual right to sound through the mask, things will again snap back into place. Then I, greatly honored and deeply thankful for this moment, shall be free not only to exchange the roles and masks that the great play of the world may offer, but free even to move through that play in my naked "thisness," identifiable, I hope, but not definable and not seduced by the great temptation of recognition which, in no matter what form, can only recognize us *as* such and such, that is, as something which we fundamentally are *not*.[13]

The Temptation of Recognition

While many of our challenges are new, most of the root causes—the temptations and pressures that shape the human heart—are quite old. In her discussion of the persona, Arendt describes the "temptation of recognition," the false belief that there is some way in which we can appear in the world and feel satisfied. There's no doubt that this temptation is nearly universal, especially when we trace that desire back a little further to (as Augustine put it) the deep restlessness of the fallen human heart: We are restless until we find our rest in him.[14]

We seek to quench that restlessness in a thousand ways, and the "temptation of recognition" is one of them. We long to be seen and affirmed. As I've already described, the modern world creates an exponentially greater sense of anxiety than any time in history. This (again) isn't to say we have it worse than ever—most Americans are generally safer from roving Cossacks and barbarians—but simply that we've exchanged some anxieties (safety from warlords, food scarcity, being eaten by wolves) for others (who am I and what am I doing with my life?).

With institutions like home, church, and nation weakened or redefined in ways that are brittle and uninformative of identity, the social realm has a compelling power for us. The desire to live as "appearing creatures"—performing, hoping to be seen and affirmed—rather than "political creatures" is a natural result of that fractured, fragile sense of identity.

Obviously, in 1975, Arendt could hardly have imagined how technology would transform the social realm. As an Arendt aficionado, I've long thought social media was far more aptly named than anyone in Silicon Valley could have imagined. It is a space of pure, empty gesture; performance and affirmation devoid of meaning and risk. And yet, in its emptiness, it is enormously powerful, offering a salve to our restlessness that, like an opiate, is powerful, short-lived, and highly addictive.

Even so, it is only the most potent expression of a much deeper phenomenon. Just as one can get "canceled" online for violating the unwritten rules of a social tribe, one can lose their membership in real-world social groups for the same reasons. Churches and religious denominations are great examples of this. When the consensus swings in one direction and an individual either doesn't get the message, doesn't understand, or disagrees, they'll face enormous pressure to conform or be expelled, and expulsion comes quickly.

To resist the pull of the crowd or mob in such a moment, one must still be able to think and judge. One has to maintain a sense of identity that isn't tied to the "temptation of recognition"—which is to say, the platform or the experience of celebrity. And the only way to find that is in solitude.

The Hard Work of Thinking

For Arendt, solitude was the primary ground of thinking, and thinking—as we've discussed—is critical if we are to remain moral actors in dark times. In *The Human Condition*, she describes thinking as a dialogue between "me and myself," which means that while "it may be the most solitary of all activities, [it] is never altogether without a partner and without company."[15]

In this dialogue between me and myself, I can come to discover what I think about something. Our metaphors for thinking often indicate this kind of internal plurality. "I'm kicking around ideas" invokes an image of several people kicking a ball back and forth from different perspectives. "I'm debating it" envisions an inner interlocutor. To talk about a "train of thought" or a "storm of ideas" presents ideas as something external to ourselves—coming from another place. Other metaphors indicate the process of thought. "Mulling something over" refers to steeping wine with spices and flavorings and, like "simmering thoughts" or a "melting pot of ideas," indicates both process and time.

Thinking, rightly understood, involves a process whereby ideas intersect, conflict, and compete (in a sense) to win *me* over to *them*. This only happens when we give time and space to the process. At times that can feel futile, and we might feel "stuck" in addressing a conflict or predicament for months on end. But most of us probably have experienced the sense of "Eureka!" that comes when, by thinking, we make sense of something that has been troubling us.

We are tempted to throw our hands up and say, "Who are we to judge?" or to parrot the judgments of others—be they demagogues, celebrities, or a social consensus. These are both thoughtless responses, but they have the strength of the mob on their side.

The alternative to these thoughtless responses is to think and judge, something more easily said than done. Most of us will experience what David Foster Wallace called "the terror of silence"[16] long before we enter solitude, and it may be the very thing that prevents us from entering it. This is actually not a fear of silence but rather a fear of the incredible noise that emerges when the surrounding world is silenced. That noise is our thoughts—our fears and anxieties. And when you've trained yourself to alleviate that noise and anxiety with busyness, distraction, and entertainment, it makes solitude and silence all the more disorienting and uncomfortable.

Those who are committed to thinking and judging will discover that it isn't a once-and-for-all activity. They will have to return to their own thoughts again and again when they run against the consensus of others, and it can feel maddening to be in the minority on a moral judgment—especially when the mob seems utterly convinced and in lockstep with one another. Thinking, in these circumstances, feels an awful lot like asking, "Am I the crazy one?"

Beth Moore at the Crossroads

Beth Moore asked that question a lot after October 2016. She was one of the Christian publishing world's most successful authors and conference speakers, and certainly one of American Christendom's most recognizable faces. She was wrapping up a speaking trip and flying home when she picked up a newspaper to read an article about Donald Trump's now-infamous *Access Hollywood* tape—the one where he boasted about how fame gave him permission to grope women.

> I'd not only seen the full transcript of Trump's off-the-air comments, I'd also read the rationalizations of multiple evangelical leaders who'd been fawning over him like he was God's gift to American Christianity. *It was just locker room talk. He's a baby Christian. He's not the same man. He made mistakes. He was just big talking like men do sometimes. Boys will be boys.*
> . . . A few voiced disgust, and I was grateful for those, but most either remained silent or actually offered excuses. Their

support for Trump's candidacy didn't appear to waver. My own brothers in the faith, who'd been easily scandalized by others, had developed a sudden and protracted case of uncharacteristic tolerance.[17]

She took to Twitter the next morning after her prayer time and posted a series of tweets addressing it head-on.

Wake up, Sleepers, to what women have dealt with all along in environments of gross entitlement and power. Are we sickened? Yes. Surprised? NO.

Try to absorb how acceptable the disesteem and objectifying of women has been when some Christian leaders don't think it's that big a deal.

I'm one among many women sexually abused, misused, stared down, heckled, talked naughty to. Like we liked it. We didn't. We're tired of it.

"Keep your mouth shut or something worse will happen." Yes. I'm familiar with the concept. Sometimes it's terrifyingly true. Still, we speak.[18]

In doing so, Moore had violated the rules of her social realm—the primary one being not to upset the happy equilibrium between political alliances, commerce, and actual evangelical conviction. As a result, Moore found herself expelled from that society.

Daily, I received word that my Bible studies were being pulled out of more churches. Some were boxed up and sent back to us. I was told some of them were burned. I expected reactions from men to the thread I'd published on social media, but I didn't see the women coming. Some of them posted pictures on social media of stacks of studies they'd thrown in the garbage, the wavy, weathered edges of the workbooks testifying to the weeks they'd spent in those pages.[19]

She was hardly alone. Many leaders of churches, denominational entities, and nonprofits found themselves disoriented by the gap between rhetoric and reality. They discovered the distinction between a movement and an institution. A movement's ideas and rhetoric will constantly morph to accommodate new facts on the ground, reshaping itself so that it can always appear true and inevitable. An institution can't change, or at least can't change quickly.

Evangelicalism, to the extent that it is an institution, has its roots in Protestant theology and a strategy of cultural engagement. To the extent that it became a movement focused on history-as-process and influencing American politics, its theological convictions were destined (like Mars Hill's) to morph and change. In the 1980s and 1990s, the movement required an emphasis on character. This could provide a contrast between evangelicals and their Democratic opponents who'd embraced the sexual revolution; it was especially convenient when doing battle with President Bill Clinton, whose dalliances were well-known long before Matt Drudge broke the Monica Lewinsky story.

In the late 2010s, in the aftermath of the Obama years, things had to change. President Barack Obama couldn't be battled on family-man credentials, and his personal faith often seemed more robust than that of his conservative opponents. In addition, the Republican Party was animated by a new spirit: rage. They were angry about the 2007 financial meltdown and the bailouts for big banks and auto manufacturers; they were angry about progressive overreach in religious liberty cases. They were angry at Mitt Romney and John McCain for losing, and angry at the liberal media for being condescending to Sarah Palin.

It's no surprise, then, that culture warriors like Newt Gingrich, Donald Trump, and Herman Cain found traction in the party when they showed they could indulge that rage. The surprise was how quickly evangelical leaders lined up to join them.

As the movement shifts, its followers shift with it. When you're primarily attached to energy and momentum, language—whether it refers to doctrine, dogma, or an articulation of the facts—is the least of your concerns. You shift quickly. Few things illustrate this so viscerally as the phrase "locker room talk."

Moore didn't shift because her attachment to the movement had been disrupted. The offense of Trump's words struck some of the deepest wounds of her life, and the cognitive dissonance of watching church leaders accommodate Trump's low character broke the spell.

In the brutal months that followed, Moore revealed (and perhaps discovered) that she'd formed an identity and a sense of conviction that ran deeper than the movement and that weren't dependent on the platforms, the conferences, or the publishers.

While I can't speak to the inner workings of her heart (though we've met, I do not know her personally), it's safe to say that Moore understood the reality described by Arendt. She knew that the stage—the temptation of recognition—was just that, a temptation, a fleeting experience, which also meant that she had a sense of personal identity beyond the stage and (more importantly) beyond the social and public realms altogether. Confronted by the *Access Hollywood* tape, she knew that she would not only have to live with the members of her audience whose experiences of abuse were being made into a mockery; she would also have to live with herself. She'd return to solitude at some point and face Beth Moore and have to explain to *her* why she'd been silent.

To put it another way, it seems to me that this moment put her own teaching to the test—namely, the core idea that ran through it all and motivated it: that being a Christian meant cultivating an intimate, personal relationship with God. This happens most powerfully when one withdraws to solitude to study the Bible and learn to pray. In this sense, one could say that all of Moore's ministry was intimately tied to the practices of solitude, and because (it turned out) she lived what she taught, she had the inner resources to think, judge, and suffer the consequences of resisting the pull of the mob in 2016.

This is not to suggest that those who chose differently don't have "quiet times" of Word and prayer, of course. But it is to say that in her case, those practices enabled her to make a judgment *different* from not only the vast majority of her fellow believers but also what the majority of her fans and followers might have expected. Not only that, Moore chose to speak publicly about that judgment, knowing that it might cost her friends, fans, and financial opportunities.

I love this example mostly because of how unexpected it was. Moore's "lane" in the Christian subculture was as mainstream as it gets. She was anything but an activist or a political commentator. She had a Texas-sized personality and the self-deprecating charm of a former aerobics teacher who'd quietly and unexpectedly become one of the world's most beloved Bible teachers. Her brilliance with metaphors and stories enabled her to connect her audience to the Bible in new ways, and that gift was both the source of her success and the object of derision (perhaps envy) from critics who labeled her a theological lightweight.

But at a time when evangelicals' convictions were tested, when they were forced to either stand by their values or stand by a morally compromised candidate who promised power, she was one of the few to stand by her values. Had she chosen to simply "go along to get along," not only would few have judged her for it, few would even have noticed that she'd never commented on the subject. It simply wasn't her style or her wheelhouse.

Her story reminds me of something Dallas Willard once said. As a young man, he'd fretted about the success and growth of his ministry. One day in prayer, he sensed God telling him,

"Dallas, never worry about having an audience; worry about having something to say."

It is in solitude, where we talk to ourselves, that we discover what we might think about anything, and it is in prayer, where we talk with God about what we—he and I—are doing together, that we cultivate that *something* to say. Moore had that *something* in 2016. While her life changed in fundamental ways, I have no doubt that history will smile on her thinking and judgment in dark times. Her witness offered a ray of hope to countless women who'd felt betrayed (and too often, betrayed *again*) by the church.

She wasn't alone, of course. I think too of my friends Joy Beth Smith and Russell Moore, whose willingness to speak out in 2016 led to equally devastating personal consequences. Or we can return to Paul Petry as an example of someone who refused to relinquish his capacity to think and judge at Mars Hill.

Each one resisted in a different way with different motivating principles and different obstacles and consequences. The common thread, though, is a sense of self that was larger than their public personae—larger than roles they played in their social realms or in their institutions. Each one had a living, breathing conscience and knew that a day would come when they'd find themselves alone with themself again. They wanted to be able to return to solitude without fear, without the anxiety of having to explain why it was that in the face of evil, they chose to say nothing or do nothing.

We desperately need to acquaint ourselves with solitude if we hope to have similar courage. We need to follow Jesus into the "lonely places" where we can think and pray and there discover our convictions. If we don't, when dark times come we'll find ourselves without words or judgments to meet the moment.

8

Storytelling and Culture Making

"How does it change?"

This question has emerged in almost every conversation I've had about the crisis in evangelicalism in the past few years. Those who are persuaded that there is indeed a crisis are eager to find a solution.

Those who aren't convinced there's a crisis often ask it cynically, as though the conditions of evangelical Christianity in the United States are inevitable. "How does it change?" is, in this case, code for "What else are we gonna do?"

The absurdity of the question reveals itself in all that has been normalized in evangelical life: celebrity pastors, spectacle-driven conferences and events, the worship-as-entertainment industry, multimillion-dollar ad campaigns for books and curricula, and so forth. To shrug and rhetorically ask, "What can one do?" assumes that this is simply how the church *must* be, that bad actors, evil behavior, and real harm are simply the cost of doing business.

So let's ask the question another way: If a robust private world of solitude and thinking is what anchors our capacity for resistance, what can flow out of solitude and make a difference in the world?

I've already offered one answer in the form of Eugene Peterson. I mentioned some of the constraining choices he made that led him away from fame and celebrity, and those are certainly critical. But they'd be hardly noteworthy if it weren't for his public life. In other words, we don't know Peterson because of his constraining choices; we know him because of his work— his translations, his teaching, his writing, and his influence on several generations of pastors and scholars. It seems safe to assume that Peterson's work will long outlive him as well as most of the work of the writers of his generation.

To understand why, look at the inextricable connection between the private and public in Peterson's work. His contribution to the world came in his words, which flowed from a life devoted to the study of language, theology, and literature. Peterson could speak artfully in his pastoral theology because he was steeped in the observations of Dickinson and Dostoyevsky. He could speak plainly in The Message because he'd imbibed the dialect of everyday people from Wendell Berry to Walker Percy. And he could speak prophetically because his love of literature let him attend to the world without being caught up in its trends, fads, and currents—to be in it but not of it.

To put it another way, Peterson's influence endures because he did excellent work. He said and wrote things that were true and beautiful, and this was the basis on which they came to the world's attention.

Contrast this with so many influential Christian authors whose success was far less about the substance of their work. Instead, they came to the world's attention either through success in other spaces (as church leaders, athletes, or social media influencers) or through the careful curation of online platforms, the formulas for which are described in half a dozen bestselling books by the gurus of "platform building." Where writing was clearly a part of Peterson's pastoral vocation, for many (most?) their books exist as pieces of a larger commercial empire or brand, and their durability—far more than their sales numbers—reveals the cold truth.

How many bestsellers will be pulped into oblivion while Peterson's *Psalms* are handed along for prayer and devotions? How many influencers will come and go while new editions of *A Long Obedience in the Same Direction* or *Under the Unpredictable Plant* or *Eat This Book* will get published?

It reminds me of Keith Richards's comments about Mick Jagger's 1985 solo album *She's the Boss*. Richards resented the album, which came about as the result of a side deal Jagger quietly made while the band was in search of a new record label. Richards thought they were better together, and he was right— *She's the Boss* was both a commercial and creative disaster. In his memoir, Richards compared it to *Mein Kampf*, admitting that he owned a copy only because "everybody owned a copy, but nobody listened to it."[1]

Richards was always the real genius of the band, an encyclopedia of the blues and a sponge who took in the influences of their peers and competitors. It was his high taste that made him jealous to keep the band together—he wanted to make art that mattered and lasted. He understood that much that happens in this world (including much of its art) is forgettable, and as much hostility and contempt as there may have been between them over the years, Richards understood it as part of the magic, part of the alchemy of The Rolling Stones. Alone, Jagger could gather an all-star cast and record *She's the Boss*, and it will stay—like Richards's copy and like mine—on the shelves. Together, they could write their timeless 1969 hit, "Gimme Shelter," a song that brought to life the tension of a world that had been torn apart by war, political assassinations, drugs, and violence. *She's the Boss* was an ego trip. "Gimme Shelter" *mattered*.

Storytelling, World Changing, and the WWE

We all know that writing songs, telling stories, and crafting beautiful words can change the world. But in the noise, hype, and media in which we all live, how does one break through?

For the innovators of the modern American megachurch, the idea seemed to be, "If you can't beat them, join them." As a result, they created a culture that trafficked in the same hype and energy, creating their own commercial and entertainment ecosystem. Maybe there's an extent to which that ecosystem is necessary. Maybe it's an artifact of the capitalist milieu that the church finds itself in.

But that doesn't mean we have to rely on that ecosystem to make an impact on the world. Indeed, it might be counterproductive to even attempt to use that ecosystem if your hope is to catalyze change or spark new ideas. The Christian ecosystem—populated as it may be by good-hearted individuals who love Jesus and want to serve the church—is not designed to provoke, rattle cages, or challenge the status quo. And when it comes to what actually grabs hold of people and makes them pay attention, the need for that artifice is probably overstated. What moves people is stories, artful performance, human drama, and connecting at the level of the heart.

I was reminded of this in the strangest way in the summer of 2023. I was listening to an episode of Brian Koppelman's podcast, *The Moment*. Koppelman is a screenwriter and a producer, and on his show he talks to other creatives about how they made their careers. The episode I heard that summer awakened my own sense of the importance of beauty in dark times, but I almost didn't listen to it. The topic held no interest to me. Frankly, I surprised myself a little when I tuned in to the episode in the first place. But I was glad I did.

So . . . let's talk about making beautiful things as an act of resistance in dark times. And let's talk about professional wrestling.

Paul Heyman is a wrestling manager. In the professional wrestling world, it's a supporting role for a wrestler that can function anywhere between a partner, a hype-man, and a mastermind who lurks in the background. Heyman looks like a Vegas pit boss with sloping shoulders, a bald head, and an expensive suit, and he is always talking and gesturing with his hands. They're huge and could just as easily hand you a crisp one-hundred-dollar bill as smack you out of your chair.

Part of the manager's role in the wrestling ecosystem is to help evolve and manipulate the plot of the stories. In years past, wrestling organizations relied on a variety of means to develop these plotlines, including publishing stories in magazines with false accounts of off-screen or off-the-mat conflicts between wrestlers. The idea, if you run the WWE, is to write a script that is somewhere between a sports story and a soap opera in order to keep tension ratcheted to a furious level so that the audience is on the edge of their seats. Heyman is extraordinarily good at this.

In an organization like the WWE, that's not always easy. There are as many as forty wrestlers in the franchise, each one nursing grudges, plotting how to backstab, and on different trajectories of hype or decline. This is, in a sense, the "art" of wrestling—not the actual events that take place in the ring but the manipulation of the crowd's desires and expectations.

And in early 2023, the WWE was in trouble.

The reigning champ was Roman Reigns, and Heyman was his "special counsel." For a long time, the storyline had been building toward a faceoff between Reigns and Cody Rhodes at WrestleMania. But in the month before the event, another wrestler—Sami Zayn—had gotten unexpected love and support from the crowd. This meant that whatever had been orchestrated for the months ahead—even if it were the most spectacular wrestling in the history of the sport—wasn't what the people wanted to see.

The WWE faced a choice. On one hand, they could have pivoted and found a way to give the people what they wanted. On the other hand, they needed to evoke the desire for the match they'd planned. To do that they had to make the conflict between Reigns and Rhodes the must-see event of 2023.

In our day and age, wrestling promotions rely on high-budget, high-production-value short films that tell the backstories, the budget of which would make most indie filmmakers blush. What makes this story noteworthy, though, is that Heyman and Rhodes chose to bypass all that and take a high-risk, low-budget, old-school approach.

Rhodes walked into the ring at the end of WWE Raw on February 6, 2023, acknowledging the elephant in the room: the crowd wanted Sami Zayn. The crowd agreed, chanting, "Sami, Sami, Sami." Rhodes began to suggest that perhaps he'd have to prove it was his time, perhaps he'd need to challenge Sami before taking on Roman Reigns. Then Heyman showed up, and his presence immediately stirred the crowd.

The entire thing is on YouTube, and even if, like me, you have no interest in wrestling, I'd encourage you to watch. It is one of the most fascinating illustrations of crowd psychology and performance art I've ever seen. Heyman is a master of the craft, controlling tone, cadence, and pathos that enables him to steer the crowd exactly where he wants them.

He began by lowering the tension, congratulating Rhodes on winning the recent Royal Rumble. Rhodes warmed up to Heyman and told a story about how in the year 2000, his dad's career as a trainer had tanked. He was making local car commercials because he was so down on his luck; it was the only way he could keep his car. But Paul Heyman found him and gave him a job, training young wrestlers at the WWE training center. It put food on the table and pride in their home again. The crowd went wild. Heyman, usually a shady, villainous type, began to weep, and the crowd chanted, "Thank you, Paul! Thank you, Paul!"

Heyman then began telling stories too, weaving a bit more tension into the room, echoing the crowd's concern that maybe Cody Rhodes had gotten ahead of himself in challenging Roman Reigns at WrestleMania. Then, like a preacher, he began running down a litany of the wrestlers Rhodes's dad, Dusty, had trained. "Your father, the American Dream Dusty Rhodes, trained and prepped Seth Rollins. Your father, the American Dream Dusty Rhodes, trained and prepped Becky Lynch. . . . Your father, the American Dream Dusty Rhodes, trained and prepped, for the highest level of success, the tribal chief, Roman Reigns. You know who your father didn't train and prep?" He paused dramatically, facing away from Cody to the crowd. "Your father did not train nor prep . . . you." With "you" he turned and pointed to Cody.

He went on to speculate why. Perhaps Dusty Rhodes wanted his son to make it in the industry without living in his father's shadow, to earn his own place. He then said this:

> God, Cody, I can't convey in words how much I loved your father. And I can tell you straight to your face, man, did your father love you. And I'll tell you this one personally. In my last conversation with your dad, he told me, you Cody, were his favorite son. But Roman Reigns was the son he always wanted.[2]

Paul then dropped the mic.

The crowd went into a rage. If Cody Rhodes had told them to burn the arena down, they'd have started tearing their seats out of the floor. Instead, he crossed the ring to Heyman, took his hand in an iron grip and said, "You know I'm just trying to win a wrestling championship and everybody . . . wants to make it personal. And that's what you just did. And you're not going to pay for it, Mr. Heyman. Your boy Roman Reigns is going to pay for it at WrestleMania when I take those titles personally."

Rhodes dropped the mic. And without adding a dollar to their production budget, the WWE had corrected course.

Storytelling as Action

You may be wondering what on earth the WWE has to do with Hannah Arendt or with the crisis of leadership among evangelicals or why I'm talking about wrestling in a chapter about culture making as an act of resistance. Believe me, no one is more surprised than I am.

But I think it's a tremendously helpful illustration of the power of what Arendt called "action"—speech and storytelling performed for the sake of changing minds. As Arendt points out, an important mimicry takes place between politics and art. When Shakespeare said that all the world was a stage and we're performers on it, he was making a political statement, not an artistic one. Those who want to change the world—or in our case, the church—have much to learn from the performing arts.

With Heyman and Rhodes, we see the power of speech and storytelling. They could have made a big-budget promo to ramp the tension back up between Rhodes and Reigns, but I doubt it would have been as effective. They also could have put out a press release making the rational, fact-driven case that it was Rhodes's turn, but it wouldn't have moved the needle at all. Fans of wrestling certainly wouldn't have gathered online or connected at work the next day to quote highlights from the press release.

Instead, two people with microphones and stories stood in front of a crowd and took them on an emotional journey. They changed their minds without ever indicating that was their task. Heyman in particular orchestrated the whole magic trick, taking one of the most primitive bonds of the human experience—the relationship of a father and son—and turning it against Rhodes: "Roman Reigns was the son I always wanted." The quote will follow Rhodes the rest of his career.

Professional wrestling is anything but high art. As WWE legend The Undertaker puts it, "Wrestling and sports entertainment is not about the moves, it really isn't. It's being able to evoke emotion in one facet or another."[3] But that only furthers my point. It is the campy, visceral aspect of wrestling, the naked absurdity of it, that allows the observer to so easily see its emotional architecture.

Watching Heyman's performance, I was reminded of Mark Antony's famous speech from *Julius Caesar*, when he turns the Roman mob against Brutus by evoking their love for Caesar and sarcastically contrasting it with the refrain, "Brutus is an honorable man."[4] Heyman's speech was meant to evoke rage, only he did so as the heel,[5] bathing in the crowd's hatred as his speech roared to its climax.

Virtuosity and Transformation

To be sure, I'm not suggesting that the way forward in dark times is to adopt the crowd control strategies of professional wrestling. Yet this story, like Brutus's speech, reveals that changing minds and hearts, even in a media-saturated age, will always be less governed by access to media, money, and spectacle, and far more governed by our understanding of human nature and our skill. The ability to persuade and motivate will depend on our "virtuosity," to use Arendt's word, to speak to and evoke the passions and desires of the crowd, regardless of our message or medium.

That kind of virtuosity is simultaneously an example of the most basic human impulse—to express ourselves—and the highest human impulse—to introduce something new into the world. Arendt calls this "action."

> With word and deed we insert ourselves into the human world, and this insertion is like a second birth, in which we confirm and take upon ourselves the naked fact of our original physical appearance. This insertion is not forced upon us by necessity . . . and it is not prompted by utility. . . . [Rather,] its impulse springs from the beginning which came into the world when we were born and to which we respond by beginning something new on our own initiative. To act, in its most general sense, means to take an initiative, to begin (as the Greek word *archein*, "to begin," "to lead," and eventually "to rule," indicates), to set something into motion (which is the original meaning of the Latin *agere*).[6]

"Action" for Arendt is any human effort carried out to change the status quo. It is political in the sense that it is public, regardless of whether it is meant to influence the state or some other institution. Action is meant to influence our shared life. It can indicate speech (words) or some kind of political mobilization (deeds), and (in my opinion) in the arts it can blur those distinctions. But the point is that a person enters the public arena with the intent to express themselves and to leave it other than how they found it.

> It is in the nature of beginning that something new is started which cannot be expected from whatever may have happened before. This character of startling unexpectedness is inherent in all beginnings and in all origins. . . . The new always happens against the overwhelming odds of statistical laws and their probability, which for all practical, everyday purposes amounts to certainty; the new therefore always appears in the guise of a miracle. The fact that man is capable of action means that the unexpected can be expected from him, that he is able to perform what is infinitely improbable.[7]

This is partially why Arendt was optimistic despite everything; there were always going to be new people born into the world, and their capacity for *action*—for doing new and unexpected things—should give us hope that whatever darkness might cloud us now will not last forever. She called this new-making quality of humanity "natality."

I think it mirrors the sentiments of Aleksandr Solzhenitsyn, who—upon receiving the Nobel Prize in Literature—took up Dostoyevsky's claim that "beauty will save the world."

> One day Dostoevsky threw out the enigmatic remark: "Beauty will save the world." What sort of a statement is that? For a long time I considered it mere words. How could that be possible? When in bloodthirsty history did beauty ever save anyone from anything? Ennobled, uplifted, yes—but whom has it saved?
>
> There is, however, a certain peculiarity in the essence of beauty, a peculiarity in the status of art: namely, the convincingness of a true work of art is completely irrefutable and it forces even an opposing heart to surrender.[8]

As Solzhenitsyn saw it, art was a great truth teller. Where a political treatise could be based on a lie, smoothing out its rough edges with polished rhetoric and subtle contradictions, a work of art based on a lie will fail.

> A work of art bears within itself its own verification: conceptions which are devised or stretched do not stand being portrayed in images, they all come crashing down, appear sickly and pale, convince no one. But those works of art which have scooped up the truth and presented it to us as a living force— they take hold of us, compel us, and nobody ever, not even in ages to come, will appear to refute them.
>
> So perhaps that ancient trinity of Truth, Goodness and Beauty is not simply an empty, faded formula as we thought in the days of our self-confident, materialistic youth? If the

tops of these three trees converge, as the scholars maintained, but the too blatant, too direct stems of Truth and Goodness are crushed, cut down, not allowed through—then perhaps the fantastic, unpredictable, unexpected stems of Beauty will push through and soar TO THAT VERY SAME PLACE, and in so doing will fulfill the work of all three?[9]

In that case, Dostoevsky's remark, "Beauty will save the world," was not a careless phrase but a prophecy.

Solzhenitsyn believed this to be true. For him, literature could uniquely tell the truth about the world, and do so in a way that stirred the heart and made the human experience plain to people across time and space.

I believe that world literature has it in its power to help mankind, in these its troubled hours, to see itself as it really is, notwithstanding the indoctrinations of prejudiced people and parties. World literature has it in its power to convey condensed experience from one land to another so that we might cease to be split and dazzled, that the different scales of values might be made to agree, and one nation learn correctly and concisely the true history of another with such strength of recognition and painful awareness as [if] it had itself experienced the same, and thus might it be spared from repeating the same cruel mistakes.[10]

Here again, it shouldn't be difficult to see the connections between the *polis* of the state and the *polis* of the church. Solzhenitsyn took up the burden of confronting Soviet totalitarianism with his own pen, telling the truth in terrible and beautiful ways. No longer could many a useful idiot glamorize communism, with the barbarism and brutality of the gulags, interrogation rooms, show trials, and mass murder laid bare.

This should be encouraging to those who feel disturbed by the state of things in the evangelical world. We face a host of powerful and wealthy institutions that don't want to tell the truth about themselves and their leaders; what Solzhenitsyn faced was far more powerful, cruel, and terrible. And he faced them with only his typewriter.

That was enough, though. By telling his story and countless other stories, he introduced something "new" into the flow of history, disrupting the status quo and inspiring countless others to find their own voices, tell the truth, and resist their own oppression. This is also part of the nature of action.

Here again, we can look to Eugene Peterson—one man, one pastor, serving a relatively small church in a world of megachurches. He bore witness to another way of doing things that by its truthfulness can cut through the noise of the age, endure passing fads, and inspire countless others to think differently about what it means to be a Christian, to be a pastor, or to be the church.

There are many others whose work belongs alongside Peterson's, offering an alternative vision of Christian faithfulness in dark times. I think of the life and work of Dallas Willard and Marva Dawn, or the work of my friends Makoto Fujimura, Steve Taylor, and Charlie Peacock who offer a countercultural witness through art and music, rarely concerned with the evangelical status quo (to the extent that they pay attention to it at all). I think of my friends at Mockingbird Ministries, steadily pointing out the strange evidences of grace among our folly, and of the writing of Robert Farrar Capon, whose love of food, beauty, and life's pleasures was matched only by his astonishment at the depths of both sin and grace. In each case, I'd argue that these souls must have all heard some version of the counsel Willard did that I mentioned already in this book: never worry about having an audience; worry about having something to say. It is the singularity of their "voice" and work that makes them stand out in our world, and by "acting," they have inspired countless others to offer their own faithful witness.

"How do we change things?" is a fair question. To answer it in Arendt's terms, we must "act." Speak. Tell stories. Do it with "excellence" and "virtuosity." Tell the truth and count on it to stand out against the distortions and lies that permeate dark times.

Each of us will hear differently the invitation to "act." We may write or paint or podcast or make films or preach—whatever it is, we do it. We might do it quietly or poorly, and we might go unnoticed for a time. That's okay. Being good at anything requires first being bad at it—and often it means being bad at it for a long time. But we do it anyway, confident that there's value in contributing our voice. Culture doesn't change any other way.

That's good news, though. It means that no matter what we're up against—whether it's a broken church, a corrupted empire, or an angry mob—we can be sure that one or two people, with nothing but a microphone and a good story, can change the world.

9

Worship, or Light in Dark Times

In 2008, Willow Creek released the *Reveal* study, one of the more fascinating episodes in recent American church history. This groundbreaking act of self-reflection came after almost thirty years of ministry, essentially daring reality to contradict the claims that Bill Hybels, the church's founder, had made from its beginning.

Willow Creek launched the seeker-sensitive model of church, programming their Sunday morning gatherings with pop music, sketches, and evangelistic messages from Hybels. During a weeknight "Deeper Life" service, another pastor would teach a more in-depth sermon accompanied by music that was more overtly worshipful and participatory. Rather than Sunday school classes, members would attend small groups in members' homes, focused on building relationships of mutual support. The church succeeded wildly and attracted tens of thousands of people. Hybels became a household name not simply because his church was successful, but because he'd established himself as an innovator in the tradition of great American entrepreneurs.

Reveal was a reckoning, though. A careful study of the transformational effect of life at Willow Creek, it was meant to expose the strengths and weaknesses of the church's ministry. Surely this legendary church's leadership had their flaws and shortcomings—the question was, What could they be? Where were the gaps in this juggernaut's armor?

Turns out, they were legion.

To put it simply, members liked Willow Creek and its programs but weren't transformed by them. Far more reliable predictors of change were spiritual disciplines such as personal Bible study and prayer. Most interesting of all, those who described themselves as deeply committed to pursuing God and serving their neighbors reported higher dissatisfaction with Willow Creek than other members.

Those conducting the survey expected to see the opposite—that the more deeply engaged a person was with the church, the more they would express affection for it. That's how consumerism generally works. The authors of *Reveal*, the book based on the study, write:

> If I drink a lot of soft drinks and my favorite is Diet Coke, my loyalty and likelihood to recommend Diet Coke to other people is extremely high. In our case, that would mean a rising level of satisfaction with the church should go hand in hand with increasing spiritual growth. Yet we found this wasn't true. Generally speaking, the higher the level of commitment to Christ, the more likely it is that the satisfaction with the church will be lukewarm.[1]

As I've already discussed, Willow Creek was driven by an ideology of leadership. Hybels's vision of the pastor as CEO and entrepreneur became the story of Willow Creek, launched a generation of imitators and a multimillion-dollar leadership conference, and sold millions of books. That success made him untouchable, leading to various abuses of power, a seriously dysfunctional culture, and a host of other issues among the staff and board.

The *Reveal* study only damns the ideology. All the cover-ups and justifications of abuse were supposedly means to a greater end—the growth of the church and advancement of the gospel through Hybels's flawed-but-successful ministry. As it turned out, that ministry wasn't successful in the most important ways. Yes, it drew a crowd and grew the organization. But those who were immersed in it ultimately weren't drawn closer to God. In fact, to those with a vibrant personal spiritual life, the church was often seen as an obstacle to growth.

As a result, Willow Creek essentially abandoned their seeker-sensitive model in 2008. Sunday morning services were programmed to help Christians seeking to grow as disciples, and the entire church had to reorient to a new way of ministry.

What didn't change? The ideology. The Willow Creek Global Leadership Summit, later rebranded as the Global Leadership Summit, continued with Hybels at the helm. He continued to tell his origin story of abandoning certain wealth and success in the marketplace in favor of ministry. And he continued to make the case that the church's real crisis was one of innovative and entrepreneurial leadership.

He wrote the foreword to the book on the *Reveal* study and published one of his own that year. It was called *Axiom*, a collection of leadership proverbs.

Painful Self-Reflection

The Willow Creek story illustrates two characteristics of ideology. The first is the power of its iron logic. Hybels had built his reputation as a leader on the effectiveness not of his preaching, nor of his personal charisma or domineering presence, but on his skills as an innovator and an organizational leader. The study presented data that really called that into question, presenting the church as an effective gatherer and keeper of crowds but not as an evangelistic or disciple-making powerhouse. Rather than argue with the data, Hybels and the other leaders at Willow Creek managed to assimilate it into the larger logic of the movement.

Consider the larger context. For almost two decades, Hybels, Willow Creek, and their allies had been combatants in the "worship wars," arguing that they'd adopted a superior model for doing evangelistic ministry in the twenty-first century. *Reveal* largely confirmed their critics, and while they were willing to accept the data and assimilate it, they did so in a way that affirmed Hybels's status as a great leader. Accepting bad news and contrary data is what great leaders do, right?

Imagine a corporation doing an audit and discovering that, for twenty years, despite public statements to the contrary, they'd been losing money. The CEO wouldn't write the foreword to the book about the audit, declaring it an act of great leadership to accept its harsh facts; he wouldn't have kept his job either.

None of this really came up for Willow Creek, though.

There's a second characteristic of ideology on display here, though, and it is on this feature that I end this book: *ideology fails*. Every time.

As a logical framework, ideology takes the shape of a system of belief. It acts like a theology, providing a syntax and vocabulary for spiritual conversations. But it doesn't teach you to pray.

A church formed around an ideology is always brittle and transactional. Friendships are oriented toward the advancement of the movement, and they tend to evaporate outside of that orienting energy. The belonging is that of a person who is riding the current of a wave or a river, but it is a restless and uncertain belonging, one that can be disorienting and uncertain; it is not the belonging that one feels when they are safe, accepted, and home.

A church built on an ideology can provide a simulacrum of spiritual experience. Being part of a movement will spike your adrenaline, stir powerful emotions, inspire ideas and fears and hopes. But of course, that isn't the same thing as encountering the presence of God. The excitement and energy of a movement has to feel expansive, just as an adrenaline junky always needs a bigger sense of risk and danger. That's why every sermon series has to be more spectacular than the last, worship "concerts" and revivals have to be more emotive and intense, and no church has ever grown big enough.

To be sure, God in his mercy can find us in these places. He can form real friendships and community within them as well. But when the leader of an ideology-driven church fails, the ideology itself proves fatally flawed. If a person wakes up to the distortions and dysfunctions of an unhealthy community, the almost universal experience of a Christian is disorientation and grief. This describes far too many Christians today, for whom the past decade of scandals has been an avalanche of heartbreak and loss.

As we seek to address that grief, we need to be sober-minded about our hopes for the future as well as the depths of our disorientation. As I've already said in this book, when looking at the dysfunctions of the modern church, it's tempting to place all the blame on abusive leaders. We know their names and stories all too well, and to be sure, they deserve due judgment for the destruction they've wrought. (If the word "judgment" bothers you, remember Peter's own words—that judgment begins with the house of God, 1 Pet. 4:17.)

And yet, if we fail to see beyond them to the larger ideological systems they inhabit, they become scapegoats and the systems remain unchanged. This was why, at the beginning

183

of *The Rise and Fall of Mars Hill*, I likened the death of the church to the plot of *Murder on the Orient Express*, in which each person bore some responsibility for a murder. One cannot blame the fall of Mars Hill solely on Mark Driscoll; one must also blame those who enabled him as well as those who accepted the status quo of a church that was formed around his ambition and ego. That implicates everyone—the fellow pastors and board members, the staff, the members, and the fans and followers around the globe.

This is an uncomfortable reality for many of us, but it's essential we own our part. We who populate dysfunctional communities, who buy the books, attend the conferences, watch the YouTube channels, and listen to the podcasts are very much a part of the problem. We create, with our presence and dollars, the possibility of all-powerful pastors. And while that is a sort of indictment all its own, it's also a key indicator of how things might change.

To borrow a phrase from a classic horror movie, the killer is inside the house. Or perhaps even better: "We have met the enemy, and the enemy is us." Our problem isn't *simply* our leaders and our institutions—though they certainly bear a share of the blame. No, the problem is *us*, more specifically our desires, which are revealed by and reflected in the kinds of churches we're building and not the other way around.

Ideology succeeds only to the extent that it satisfies a certain set of desires in us; so long as those desires remain, we are likely to repeat our institutional mistakes. Ideology fails, ultimately, because a point will come where its ability to absorb facts reaches its limit. Like tempered steel, it is unyielding and unbending, crushing much in its path. But eventually reality becomes too much to consume, where it meets forces more powerful than the jaws of its logic, and it will shatter as a result. This sometimes is sparked by the failure of a leader—exposing the flaws in the ideology they embody. It will sometimes come in the slow drip of systemic collapse, where an institution's ability to cover up failure or project an idyllic self-image can't be sustained against the steady flow of stories that expose hypocrisy and lies.

In the disillusionment that follows the collapse of a community or the loss of a dream, our greatest danger is to be seduced by another ideology. We go from one all-consuming, all-explaining idea to another, perhaps embodied in another movement-oriented evangelical community or in an ideology of deconstruction or activism. Whatever the case, we will be tempted to recover our sense of the world's comprehensibility, and if we indulge that temptation, we will be led tragically astray.

No Substitute for Transcendence

I'm reminded of a metaphor that Hannah Arendt used often. Even in her day, people liked to talk about the temptation to replace the role of religion in a person's life with politics. She likened the distinction between them to the difference between a shoe and a hammer. One can certainly drive a nail into a wall with a shoe, she said, but that did not mean it was a suitable substitute for a hammer, far less that it was an actual hammer.[2]

Politics can't substitute for religion because it *isn't* religion. Even at its most ideological, politics properly understood is about the relationships between men or women and their neighbors; it is not about the pursuit of the divine, transcendence, or the ultimate sources of meaning and purpose in life. One's religious beliefs will often provide a foundation for their politics, but that only further emphasizes the distinction between the categories.

For instance, in the Judeo-Christian tradition, the value of human life is paramount in all of creation since humanity is made in the image of God. That idea undergirds our political

185

decisions and could give shape to convictions about everything from school lunch programs to immigration to abortion policy. A wise person understands the distinction between first-order religious convictions and the political implications. They should see a difference between the meaning found in pursuing political goals (creating a more just world, for instance) and religious ones (living in harmony with the will of God).

We've already discussed the ways that rootlessness and the loss of transcendence make us more susceptible to ideology, promising purpose through immanent means ("advancing the kingdom through the local church"). By recognizing that a shoe is not a hammer—that politics isn't religion or, in this case, that an ideology isn't the mission of God—we can begin to find our way back to those first-order questions of meaning and purpose.

In other words, we need something better and more beautiful than what ideology offers. This is true not only because ideology creates the conditions for abuse and destruction, but more fundamentally because it cannot satisfy our deepest human needs. The cry of the soul is not to be a "fully engaged" member of the local church; it's not to be a "real man" or "real woman" in a "real marriage." It's also not to use our spiritual gifts, find our calling, master this or that method of discipleship, or successfully become a "multiplying" Christian.

Rather, the cry of the soul is to come home to God. "Come to me," Jesus said, "all who are weary and burdened, and I will give you rest" (Matt. 11:28). Augustine said that we are restless until we find our rest in God.[3] This is why ideology *must* fail. Even the good it promises—utopian community, identity, belonging, or purpose—cannot substitute for what the heart most wants. And as the Scriptures make so clear, there's an inversion of desire in coming home to God that ideology cannot compare with. Though my heart and flesh may fail, though those I love might abandon me, though I might lose all I have, if I can remain in the presence of God, I will keep my satisfaction and joy.

Worship as Homecoming

To frame all of this theologically, recovering from the ideological distortions of modern evangelicalism means rightly orienting our hearts. In other words, it is a matter of worship. The word itself helps to clarify what I mean: "worship" comes from the Old English word *weorþ*, meaning "worth" or "value." To worship something is simply to ascribe it worth. In this, it first and foremost means (as Augustine described it so well) rightly ordering our loves. This includes constraining our love for lesser goods—including those goods that come from belonging to a community, a church, or a movement. It means recognizing and fiercely guarding the beauty, goodness, and worthiness in knowing God.

Once we recognize that coming home to God is a matter of worship, we'll begin to see that the temptations of ideology are a form of worship as well. Seen through the lens of worship, we discover that ideology is idolatry—falsely ascribing worth to things that cannot satisfy. Consider ideology's characteristics: it makes a false promise, demands total allegiance and sacrifice, and consumes those who devote themselves to it. This is the classic description of idolatry—a dead vessel made by human imagination that one bows to and cries out, "Save me, you are my God." It cannot see you or hear you, much less love you or save you.

Consider the fall of some of evangelicalism's bright lights. Wasn't the caricature of masculinity espoused by Driscoll—especially its combination of combativeness and certainty—the very thing that led to his downfall? Wasn't there something about Hybels's vision of exceptional leadership that made room for the exceptions he indulged?

This is the nature of idols: they entice us with a promise, we pour our lives out in service and pursuit of them, and in the end, they crush us. It's as true for leaders as it is for followers. Whether we're talking about a vision of masculinity, entrepreneurial leadership, or a specific, branded vision of mature Christianity, when we conflate these experiences and goals with the all-satisfying promise of communion with God, we are being seduced by false gods.

Thinking in terms of worship also helps us to address the challenges of the modern world, such as the loss of roots and wings. What can satisfy the wandering soul? How can we calm the anxieties that accompany a brittle and unstable identity? There are answers that institutional leaders should consider, all the way from the nation to the neighborhood association. But "fixing" these problems will take generations. What do we do in the meantime? The clearest answer, rooted deep in the Scriptures, is to invite the world to worship the living God and to see his beauty revealed in the face of Jesus.

This, of course, means far more than just singing a few songs on a Sunday morning or buying a $150 ticket to see a famous worship leader at your local concert arena. Unfortunately, over the last thirty years, worship's definition has been narrowed in such a way as to make most people think only in terms of music. For many, it refers exclusively to music, and to a specific genre of music at that: the emotive, contemporary pop of Hillsong, Elevation, and a half dozen other well-known Christian artists. This reveals not so much a problem with music or worship as a poverty of language and imagination.

But thankfully, that is easily overcome.

Even a cursory reading of the Gospels reveals a picture of worship that is far more than singing. Rather, it's a life lived unto God in "Spirit and truth." Perhaps no one has better articulated that vision than Harold Best did in his book *Unceasing Worship*. He described the fundamental human attribute of "continuous outpouring"—the need of men and women to pour out their lives in service or praise of some greater good. This helps us understand not only that we were "made to worship" (as several contemporary worship songs remind us) but also that the heart is an "idol factory" (as John Calvin once said).[4]

David Foster Wallace, speaking as someone who was deeply skeptical of all religion, said something quite similar:

> In the day-to-day trenches of adult life, there . . . is no such thing as not worshipping. Everybody worships. The only choice we get is what to worship. And an outstanding reason for choosing some sort of God or spiritual-type thing to worship—be it J.C. or Allah, be it Yahweh or the Wiccan mother-goddess or the Four Noble Truths or some intangible set of ethical principles—is that pretty much anything else you worship will eat you alive. . . . If they are where you tap real meaning in life—then you will never have enough. Never feel you have enough. It's the truth.
>
> Worship your own body and beauty and sexual allure and you will always feel ugly, and when time and age start showing, you will die a million deaths before they finally plant you. . . . Worship power—you will feel weak and afraid, and you will need ever more power over others to keep the fear at bay. Worship your intellect, being seen as smart—you will end up feeling stupid, a fraud, always on the verge of being found out.[5]

Ideology could not exist apart from this made-to-worship aspect of human nature, catching us in the momentum of a grand story, calling us to sacrifice for a greater purpose, and threading us along toward ever-increasing self-sacrifice and continuous outpouring toward that goal. There is nothing that ideology won't demand—money, family, morality—in service of a greater good.

189

The difference between ideology and real religious experience is that the former offers nothing in return, whereas the latter is life-giving even as it invites us to pour ourselves out as a "living sacrifice." A rightly ordered heart will "run and not grow weary, . . . walk and not be faint" (Isa. 40:31).

The World That Worship Makes Accessible

Practically speaking, the difference between worship and ideology—which is to say, the gap between worship and idolatry in the modern world—is the difference between the worlds of the poet who wants to stick his head into the heavens and the rationalist who wants to cram the heavens into his head.[6] In other words, worship always invites us into something larger than ourselves, a bigger cosmos, a bigger story, a more wondrous and mysterious gospel, and a more beautiful Savior than the ones we knew before.

Worship ought to be an experience like Job's encounter with God in the whirlwind, who compounds and expands mysteries rather than resolves them. Contrast that with many contemporary worship experiences. They may indeed involve real beauty and creativity and might powerfully stir our affections and emotions, but they are also entirely comprehensible. It is easy to point to the skill of the worship leaders and preachers, the effects of the architecture and technology, the physical appearance of the people on stage, and the emotive qualities of the songs and stories as the source of whatever experience we may have had at a church gathering.

This can be true regardless of one's tradition. In contemporary worship services, one encounters beautiful people with perfect teeth, lasers and fog machines, and swelling pop music that evokes a desired effect. In traditional services, it might come through vestments, incense, and a two-million-dollar pipe organ. The point isn't to condemn these cultural artifacts or standards absolutely but to question what they are in service to. They function as a kind of iconography—a window into the good life available to the faithful of the community. What is that good life? What is on display? What is the invitation?

For far too many evangelical communities, the good life on display is a commodified vision and is often some variation of the American dream. At Mars Hill, it was (as Driscoll often put it) a guy covered in tattoos with a Bible in one hand and a baby in the other. At Willow Creek, it was an expensive golf polo, a full Rolodex, and a sizable 401(k). Increasingly today, the good life on display at churches looks like that of an Instagram influencer, a life of excessive self-display and aesthetic beauty as well as the aesthetic trappings of upper-middle-class consumerism.

These are visions that fit into the rationalist's head. They're comprehensible and achievable, and if history is any indication, they'll successfully grow a church—for a while. But because they do not ultimately bring us home to God, they are not built to last. The good life they offer cannot provide meaning and purpose during times of suffering and grief, and the bonds they form prove brittle when tested.

This proves all the more true when we understand worship as an all-of-life reality. There is a kind of symbiotic relationship between the "scattered" life lived unto God out in the world and the "gathered" practices of the local church. There's an obvious primacy to the gathered church—most self-evidently in the fact that most churches limit the celebration of baptism and the Lord's Supper to formal worship services. These gatherings are where we imbibe the language, metaphors, and images that inform how we think, pray, and imagine our spiritual lives elsewhere.

Examine our gatherings, then, and you'll quickly discover whether they make our spiritual world larger or smaller. Does gathered worship make God more grand, more mysterious, or less? Does the vision of the spiritual life displayed in our gatherings feel like an open world, where God meets different people with different gifts and leads them to different expressions of faithful Christian life? Or does it feel like a closed world, where faithful discipleship means becoming an intellectual and emotional facsimile of someone else's faith? Does a person leave church gatherings thinking more wondrously about God's being, his nature, his kindness and grace, or do they leave thinking more anxiously or seriously or intensely about becoming the right kind of person, according to the vision of the good life that was on display for an hour?

Who is the hero of our gatherings? Is it the God who saves, or is it the pastor, the worship leader, or you—the church member who must be the hero of your family or workplace?

How is the church described in our gatherings? Is it the people of God who gather at all times and in all places? Or is the church seen as confined to this local expression?

Practically speaking, are our gatherings places where those who come with sorrows will feel as welcomed, heard, and understood as those who come with joys?

Here's a thought experiment for your next church service. Imagine a couple who attend the service together. They've been married twenty-five years, and they've been fighting for six months. After the service, they go to lunch, and the husband drops dead in his mashed potatoes. Will his wife be better prepared for that moment because she went to church that morning, or would it have been better if she'd skipped? To borrow my friend John Witvliet's phrase: Will worship have formed her for her "encounter with death"?

I want to resist going much further for fear that I'll say more than is helpful. The essential point is made: worship should, to paraphrase Obi-Wan Kenobi, invite us into a larger world. Ideology will always shrink our world in order to make it manageable, comprehensible, and achievable. In doing so, it produces results—energy, crowds, movements—but it does not bring us home.

We're left with something frail and unmanageable as an alternative. We find ourselves at the mercy of God who is like the wind—unpredictable in his coming and going, undeniably present but beyond our human grasp.

For a long time, as a pastor of worship (a job I held for fifteen years), I really believed that my job involved a kind of spiritual two-step. I had to produce a service of liturgical and musical excellence, and then it was up to God to "finish" the work by writing it on people's hearts. I was constrained by his willingness to finish what I began; he was constrained by whether I put good offerings on the table—good raw material.

Over the years, I discovered people walking away with messages (for good or ill) that were wholly unintended by our services. I also saw services that were the absolute peak of what our team of musicians and artists were capable of fall entirely flat. I eventually began to realize that I didn't know what was happening in those gatherings.

A little later, I noticed something else. In moments of crisis, the language of worship would appear in the stories, prayers, and encouragements of our members. A regular prayer we'd stolen from Cranmer or one of the Puritans would pop up at a hospital bedside. Lyrics from Wesley or Watts would show up in text messages when someone shared bad news. The language of worship was an architecture on which daily experience could be hung in a way that made sense of it.

For that to happen, worship had to be larger than life, not as a matter of production or musical execution but conceptually. Worship had to describe the breadth of human experience and promise the presence of a God who was big enough to hold all of it together. The church had to be part of a continuum that extended long before us and would continue long after us.

There was room for the local, for the particular, to matter. There was room for the church to have a sense of calling and purpose in the community as well. But that sense of particularity and calling was a smaller story that fit inside something much more universal, eternal, and cosmic.

To embrace the greater story probably won't require hiring consultants, rewriting polity documents, or starting from scratch. It likely won't mean changing denominations, tossing out your commitment to orthodoxy, or nailing anything to anybody's front door. But it will likely mean a serious commitment to the other ideas I've described in part 2 of the book—a commitment to silence and solitude, to thinking, to imagination and creativity, and to real friendships. It will require a spirit of repentance instead of grandiosity, patience instead of urgency, and mystery rather than certainty and comprehensibility.

The Consolations of Judgment Day

I'll never forget a conversation a few years ago with an older pastor. He'd been serving his church for three decades and had seen it through a number of trials and controversies. I'd been asking him about one of them—not directly related to his congregation but one involving a younger pastor he'd known and with whom he'd been occasionally associated.

As we talked, a variety of scandals came up, many of which he'd witnessed up close. Many of these leaders had self-immolated in their ministries. Then, with little in the way of repentance or restitution, they had started over again to great fanfare and success. I asked my friend how he kept his own head in the game, and how he hadn't grown cynical after the series of failures that had occurred before his eyes.

He sighed and said, "Because I believe in God. I believe in the wisdom of God, the judgment of God, and the love of God." He went on to talk about how his confidence in God's judgment relieved him from a sense of anxiety about evil in the world; God wasn't responsible for that evil, but he would ensure justice was eventually carried out. He also spoke of his confidence in God's ultimate kindness to those he loves.

He paused a moment before adding, "And I believe I'm one of them. I believe he loves me, and that's enough to keep going."

He could have offered me a strategy for resisting cynicism or articulated a leadership philosophy that made him resilient. But instead, he talked about God and the attributes of God that enable him to trust him through thick and thin. He said it all not as a sermon but as an act of worship.

In Matthew 5:14–16, Jesus told his followers they were like a city on a hill that cannot be hidden, and to let their light shine before others. This passage seems especially poignant when directed at a church in dark times, where too often the talk of light is accompanied by the phrase, "Sunlight is the best disinfectant."

It raises the question: What is light in dark times? Is there more that can be done to shine light in dark places, to expose what's hidden and confront what's evil?

The answer is yes. It's to worship, to reveal God in our gathered and scattered lives as more beautiful than the world had ever hoped or imagined, and to tell them that this God is inviting them home.

It's a message for us as much as it's a message for anyone. For many of us who've seen the church's dark underbelly, who've been infected by its rot, or who have watched friends and loved ones suffer under the leadership of evil men, it's a message we need more desperately than ever.

God loves us and invites us home. It is a simple but incomprehensible truth, a story that will never grow old. We need not fear growing tired of telling it or fear that people will grow tired of hearing it. There is no better story, no better path to belonging, and no brighter light for dark times.

AFTERWORD

Reading Arendt in Jerusalem

It's late on a Friday, and as I type I'm breaking the Sabbath. Every keystroke sends a series of sparks through this laptop, and according to Jewish tradition, making a spark—no matter how microscopic—is akin to kindling a fire, which is expressly banned in Exodus 35:1–3. The more obvious violation is that I am writing, which for me is work, and there is no ambiguity about work being banned on Shabbat.

Normally, none of this would cross my mind, but tonight I am in Jerusalem, and Shabbat cannot be avoided in Jerusalem.

A few hours ago, I stood with a crowd of mostly ultra-Orthodox Jews at the Western Wall of the Temple Mount. They wrapped their arms and foreheads with tefillin and chanted, sang, and wept their prayers. Some covered their heads with prayer cloths. Others sang horas and clapped their hands and danced.

Among the Haredim are others, all wearing kippahs, many in the uniform of the Israeli Defense Forces. They have assault rifles on their shoulders. A few have far-off looks in their eyes. Others are excited. Most look no older than my teenage daughter.

I've been to the Western Wall many times, and tonight the crowd is small. Like all of Jerusalem this week, it feels haunted. The shops are closed. The Church of the Holy Sepulchre is as empty as the tomb of Jesus, and everywhere are reminders that Israel is a nation at war.

It's a little more than a month after the massacre that Israelis have been calling the Black Sabbath. On October 7, 2023, Hamas terrorists streamed across the border from Gaza and unleashed a day of barbarism, rape, and murder that left more than 1,200 people dead. They kidnapped almost 250 more, including Holocaust survivors and infants.

In the time since, Israel began an unprecedented campaign against Hamas in Gaza, promising to end their capacity to threaten Israelis again. And around the world, from Ivy League college campuses to global cities, protests against the war and against the very existence of Israel have erupted.

In Los Angeles, a man died from a blunt force head injury while counterprotesting against Hamas sympathizers. In New York, at Cooper Union College, a group of students locked themselves in a library to protect themselves from a mob. At a Russian airport in Dagestan, a near pogrom erupted after rumors had spread that Jewish refugees were on a recently landed plane. In Tunisia, a mob burned a synagogue to the ground after a rocket strike on a Gaza hospital was falsely blamed on Israel. Footage of protesters outside the Sydney Opera House showed them apparently chanting "gas the Jews" and other anti-Semitic horrors. Around the globe, passersby are ripping down posters of kidnapped Israeli children at bus stops and intersections, calling the posters propaganda.

I've spent much of my adult life reading Hannah Arendt and studying World War II. My interest in the malforming power of ideology has led me to read far more about the history of anti-Semitism than most people, and yet still I am stunned by these recent events.

As one Jewish friend put it, "Every day is Purim now, and every Jew is Esther—begging the world for the right to defend ourselves from those who want to wipe us off the face of the earth." Another said he has had to reckon with a warning from his mother from decades ago. "She warned me, when I got into academia, not to let myself believe I was one of them. 'To them,' she said, 'you'll always be a Jew.' I thought she was a cynic; it turns out she was right."

To be sure, I'm not suggesting that all criticism of Israel is anti-Semitic, nor is all of the antiwar sentiment that has arisen since October 7 anti-Semitic. You'll be hard-pressed to find an Israeli who *doesn't* have something critical to say of their government—especially the current right-wing coalition that came to power this year. But when the line is crossed from criticizing the state's policies to questioning its right to exist, when a nation founded in poverty by refugees from Europe, Russia, Ethiopia, Iraq, Iran, and Yemen is labeled a "settler-colonial state," or when an ethical or judicial standard is demanded of that state that is not demanded of any other nation, you've crossed into anti-Semitism. As I write this, that line is being crossed constantly.

As my friend Robert Nicholson puts it, anti-Semitism is ultimately a hatred of "chosenness,"[1] which is to say it is a hatred of the love, mercy, and redemptive work of God in a fallen world. Such hatred drove the enemies of Israel throughout the Old Testament, and in the two millennia since the resurrection, it remains a corruption of the gospel.

When Jesus became flesh, he took on Jewish flesh, the son of a Jewish mother. His Scriptures, his liturgies, his celebrations, and his traditions were Jewish. To hate Jews is to hate Jesus, and for Satan and the principalities and powers of the world, that is precisely the point. Anti-Semitism is the "oldest hatred," and every year Jews pray the Vehi Sheamda at Passover, which includes this passage:

> For not only one (enemy) has risen up against us to destroy us,
> but in every generation they rise up to destroy us.
> But the Holy One, Blessed be He, delivers us from their hands.

I knew and believed all of this before October 7, but I was not prepared to behold it with my own eyes.

The Vehi Sheamda recognizes that new enemies emerge in every generation, which is why October 7 is a shock. The particular hatred, motivations, tactics, and desires of Hamas are surprising and new. A world that had been warned about gas chambers and *Einsatzgruppen* wasn't prepared for the butchering of Jews to be live streamed on Telegraph, TikTok, and Facebook.

What anti-Semitic ideologies hold in common, though, is the "key to history" at the heart of their worldviews. Hamas's vision for a Palestine free from Jews "from the river to the sea" echoes Adolf Hitler's vision of a Europe made *judenrein*—free of Jews. These ideologies held out Jews as the source of the historic troubles for their people, and in so doing, created a plausible framework to call for their mass murder.

Like Nazi ideology (which simplistically blamed Jews for all woes), modern anti-Semitism ignores the complicating factors that led to Palestinian suffering. It ignores the responsibilities of UN states that partitioned the land, the rejection of the Palestinian people by the Arab armies that went to war in 1948 and 1967, and the decades of theft, corruption, and lies of the leaders of Palestinian terror organizations—including Hamas's leadership, who live as the billionaire guests of the Qataris and have experienced none of the burden or risk of the citizens of Gaza during their eighteen-year campaign of terror. Ideology blinds.

An entirely different ideology animates their coagitators on the campuses of elite universities, where Israel is the "European settler-colonialist" oppressor that has victimized indigenous Palestinians. These protesters flatten the complex history of Jewish resettlement, Palestinian identity, and postwar geopolitics into a simplistic narrative of "victims" and "oppressors." Here we see again how ideology bends reality. It doesn't matter that a majority of Israeli Jews are descendants of refugees from Arab and African nations like Iraq, Iran, Morocco, and Ethiopia, and not Europe. It doesn't matter that 20 percent of Israeli citizens are not Jews but nonetheless have full rights as citizens, including the ability to vote, serve in the government, and serve in the military.

Nor do the many details of peacemaking efforts or the general posture of Israelis toward a two-state solution matter to those chanting "Globalize the Intifada" and "There is only one solution." Ideology has long won the day, suspending many people's capacity for thinking, creating a sense of movement, morality, and belonging. It is the energy of the mob that excites and animates far more than the facts of anyone's suffering.

To be sure, ideology exists on the Israeli side too, particularly among the militant right. Their antagonisms and provocations are problematic in their own way, and their ideology contains the seeds of destruction and violence. But it would be an exaggeration to suggest that the Black Sabbath was the result of these provocations, since Hamas has made it clear that the provocation for October 7 was the presence of Jews in historic Israel.

The common thread of all ideology is its dehumanizing tendency. I came here to Israel in the midst of this war to try and resist the dehumanization on both sides of the conflict and to explore the role of both ideology and religious desire in shaping the politics and conflicts of this tiny state that holds so much power in the modern imagination. By the time this book releases, you'll be able to judge for yourself whether I made sense of any of it.

But tonight, I am bewildered. I'm bewildered by the spectacle of terror and death. I'm bewildered by the absurdity of ideological snares and by the providence of God. I've walked through homes, bedrooms, and nurseries in the aftermath of an unspeakable massacre. I've sheltered from rockets in Ashkelon. I've heard Jews, Muslims, and Christians talk about the end of the world or matters of eschatological importance with startling immediacy.

What I love about Jerusalem is what makes it such a terrifying place. So much of modernity's power evaporates here. The world's lack of transcendence, the sense of disconnect from spirituality, tradition, and story—none of that works in a city where you can walk, in a matter of minutes, from a shrine that covers the Foundation Stone, where Abraham once laid his son Isaac and prepared to sacrifice him, to the shrine of the cross, where Golgotha is still visible beneath the hulking, medieval structure of the church. It is a city that turns the tables on the inner skeptic, where the weight of history is on the side of the Bible, and where doubts are contested by the material world.

After welcoming Shabbat at the Western Wall tonight, I walked back from the Old City to my hotel nearby. On the way, I passed the King David Hotel, where Arendt stayed when she came here in 1961. Just a few kilometers down the road is the Supreme Court of Israel, where she watched Adolf Eichmann's trial.

I think of her constantly here, wondering what she'd make of the mountaintop settler I met in the West Bank, the Muslim scholar and member of the Waqf who served us chocolate-covered dates, the Bedouin woman who served us her impossibly thick coffee while describing sheltering from the attacks in her home in Rahat. Arendt liked people and ideas, and I imagine her being engrossed here. Her own opinions on Zionism shifted over the years, and she was disturbed by the treatment of Palestinians. But I can also imagine that she might have had some invective for the ideologies of Hamas and the campus left.

When the Black Sabbath attacks happened, I was putting together the final chapters of this book. I must admit that for a few days, I wondered whether I should publish it at all. I was very late in submitting the manuscript (as I tend to be), and yet I would come to the computer and open the manuscript but quickly find myself scrolling social media, texting friends or family in Israel, obsessing over the grim news as it trickled out. I began to wonder if what the world really needed now was a fresh take on Arendt's wisdom on the nature of anti-Semitism and the banality of evil—not an attempt to expand her thesis into this new territory. And yet I can't help seeing how it's all tied together.

In the end, ideology is modernity's fruit of the tree of the knowledge of good and evil. It promises us the ability to know good from evil and become like God, pointing the way for us to usher in utopia by acts of our own will. All we have to do is implement our key to history—and crush whatever or whoever might stand in our way.

Such ideology can bring devastation to body and soul, and perhaps the greater reason for moving forward with this book is the recognition—now on display in vivid detail—that ideas have consequences and that when we see people as means or obstacles to our utopian goals, we make extraordinary evil possible.

From my seat by this hotel window, I can't see what the world will look like when this book comes out several months from now. I pray the war will be over and that by some miracle there will be a new peace for this region and the world. I've been struck by the comment of one Israeli to that end: "We just have to trust that when Messiah comes, he'll bring the peace we all want—the Jews, the Israelis, the Muslims, the Christians, the Palestinians." I couldn't help but smile and in my heart echo the prayer the apostle John prayed on the island of Patmos, found in Revelation 22:20:

Amen. Come, Lord Jesus.

Mike Cosper
Jerusalem, November 17, 2023

ACKNOWLEDGMENTS

My friend Alan Noble often says, "Writing a book is impossible. No one has done it." I think he's right. It certainly feels that way in the middle of a project. It can feel that way at the end too, when the manuscript is in your hands and you wonder how on earth it came into being. This book feels that way. And yet, here it is.

This book would not exist if it weren't for Jay Barry, my college philosophy professor whose affection for Arendt led to my own. I've learned from countless others over the years, but the experience of your classroom, more than any other, shaped my moral and ethical thinking for the past twenty-five years by challenging me to think and teaching me to make someone like Arendt (or Heidegger or Foucault) an intellectual partner and not an adversary. Thanks as well to Roger Berkowitz at the Arendt Center at Bard College for being an encourager and friend and for answering my unsolicited questions over the years.

Thanks to my colleagues and conversation partners at *Christianity Today*, especially Erik Petrik, Matt Stevens, Russell Moore, Nicole Martin, Clarissa Moll, and Tim Dalrymple.

Thanks to my editor, Katelyn Beaty, for your patience with this project. I am reminded that the King James translation renders "patience" as "long suffering," even as I am reminded of the great Douglas Adams quote: "I love deadlines. I love the whooshing sound they make as they go by." Genuinely, I owe you a debt, and I am incredibly grateful for your interest in and faith in this project.

Thanks to Don Gates, Joel Lawrence, Kevin Jamison, Eric Johnson, Scott Slucher, and countless others who have helped me refine these ideas over the years.

Thanks to Sarah, Dorothy, and Maggie Cosper. I promise to change the subject now that this book is done.

Most of all, I am thankful to Hannah Arendt herself, who I'm sure would have a bone or two to pick with my thinking. It is a Jewish tradition to remember the dead by saying, "May their memory be a blessing." In this case, having had my own thoughts haunted by Hannah Arendt for more than two decades, that is certainly true. Her memory is a blessing, and I am grateful.

NOTES

Introduction

1. Hannah Arendt referred to the Nazi death camps as "corpse factories," which rightly frames them as products of modernity and the Industrial Revolution. It's my intent to say something similar about our broken religious institutions, whose uncritical adoption of ideology as a substitute for theology and thinking has made them trauma factories. See Hannah Arendt, *The Origins of Totalitarianism* (New York: Meridian, 1958), 459.

2. Hannah Arendt, "'What Remains? The Language Remains': A Conversation with Günter Gaus," in *The Portable Hannah Arendt*, trans. Joan Stambaugh, ed. Peter Baehr (New York: Penguin, 2003), 8–9.

3. Hannah Arendt, letter to Karl Jaspers, quoted in Samantha Rose Hill, *Hannah Arendt* (London: Reaktion, 2021), 162.

4. Arendt, quoted in Marie Luise Knott, ed., "Letter 132, June 23, 1963," in *The Correspondence of Hannah Arendt and Gershom Scholem* (Chicago: University of Chicago Press, 2017), 454. I'll have a lot more to say about this conflict in a later chapter.

5. Hannah Arendt, *The Human Condition*, 2nd ed. (Chicago: University of Chicago Press, 2018), 248.

Author's Note: Dark Times and Godwin's Law

1. Hannah Arendt, *The Origins of Totalitarianism* (New York: Meridian, 1958), 459.

Chapter 1 Exchanging the Truth for a Lie

1. Mark Driscoll, "Fathers and Fighting," sermon, September 30, 2007, Mars Hills Church, Seattle, Washington, available at http://marshill.info/marshill/media/nehemiah.

2. Mark Driscoll, quoted in "The Brand," *Rise and Fall of Mars Hill* (podcast), episode 6, August 2, 2021, https://www.christianitytoday.com/ct/podcasts/rise-and-fall-of-mars-hill/rise-fall-mars-hill-podcast-mark-driscoll-brand.html.

3. They've documented their story in fine detail online at wwwjoyfulexiles .com, including nearly six months' worth of written communication between them and the Mars Hill elders. I also covered it more extensively on episode 7 of *The Rise and Fall of Mars Hill.*

4. Reported by PARSE editors, "Mars Hill Elders' Letter of Confession," *Christianity Today*, November 2, 2014, https://www.christianitytoday.com/pastors /2014/november-online-only/mars-hill-elders-public-confession-meyer-petry.html.

5. Jamie Munson, letter to Paul Petry, October 1, 2007, available at https:// joyfulexiles.com/wp-content/uploads/2012/03/10-01-2007-termination-ltr -jamie-munson.pdf.

6. The publication of his "Black Notebooks" in 2014 demonstrated significantly more anti-Semitic sentiment than previously known, largely putting to rest defenses of Heidegger that argued he had no choice but to be enthusiastic about Hitler.

7. Hannah Arendt, *Essays in Understanding, 1930–1954: Formation, Exile, and Totalitarianism* (New York: Schocken, 2005), 6.

8. Alexis de Tocqueville, *Democracy in America* (New York: Alfred Knopf, 1945), 2:331.

9. Hannah Arendt, *The Origins of Totalitarianism* (New York: Meridian, 1958), 459.

10. Arendt, *Origins of Totalitarianism*, 468.

11. Arendt, *Origins of Totalitarianism*, 469.

12. Arendt, *Origins of Totalitarianism*, 470–71.

13. Arendt, *Origins of Totalitarianism*, 470.

14. Arendt, *Origins of Totalitarianism*, 469.

15. Aleksandr Solzhenitsyn, *The Gulag Archipelago* (New York: Harper-Collins, 2007), 1:173–74.

16. Also published as *Demons* or *The Devils*.

17. Hannah Arendt, "The Possessed," in Arendt, *Thinking without a Banister: Essays in Understanding, 1953–1975* (New York: Schocken, 2018), 363.

18. Hannah Arendt, 1967 notes for a lecture on Dostoyevsky's *The Possessed*, in Hannah Arendt Papers, container 69, quoted in James Bernauer, "Bonhoeffer and Arendt at One Hundred," *Studies in Christian-Jewish Relations* 2, no. 1 (2007): 77–85.

19. David Foster Wallace, *Infinite Jest* (New York: Little, Brown, 2007), 899.

20. Hannah Arendt, *The Human Condition*, 2nd ed. (Chicago: University of Chicago Press, 2018), 5.

21. Hannah Arendt, *Eichmann in Jerusalem: A Report on the Banality of Evil* (New York: Penguin, 2006), 202–3.

22. Arendt, *Eichmann in Jerusalem*, 203.

Chapter 2 The Birth of Ideology and the Comprehensible World

1. It's been more than twenty years since I attended this event, and while aspects of this are vivid, it is nonetheless a distant memory recalled to the best of my ability.

2. This is my word, not hers. She focuses more on the universal perspective, which I include as part of this conversation but not as central to it.

3. This is the subject of chapter 6 in Hannah Arendt, *The Human Condition*, 2nd ed. (Chicago: University of Chicago Press, 2018).

4. Arendt, *Human Condition*, 249.

5. Arendt, *Human Condition*, 250.

6. Arendt, *Human Condition*, 251.

7. Arendt, *Human Condition*, 248.

8. *Oppenheimer*, directed by Christopher Nolan, Universal Pictures, 2023.

9. Arendt, *Human Condition*, 260, quoting Galileo.

10. Arendt, *Human Condition*, 254.

11. Paul Ricoeur, *Freud and Philosophy: An Essay on Interpretation* (New Haven: Yale University Press, 1970), 32.

12. Arendt, *Human Condition*, 262.

13. Hannah Arendt, *On Revolution* (New York: Penguin, 2006), 36.

14. Alexis de Tocqueville, *Democracy in America* (Chicago: University of Chicago Press, 2000), 7.

15. Hannah Arendt, *Between Past and Future: Eight Exercises in Political Thought* (New York: Penguin, 2006), 81.

16. Arendt, *Between Past and Future*, 81.

17. Arendt, *Between Past and Future*, 63, 64.

18. *Veep*, season six, episode 10, "Groundbreaking," aired June 25, 2017, on HBO, written and directed by David Mandel.

19. Bill Hybels, quoted in "State of Emergency," *Rise and Fall of Mars Hill* (podcast), episode 7, August 9, 2021, https://www.christianitytoday.com/ct/podcasts/rise-and-fall-of-mars-hill/mars-hill-mark-driscoll-podcast-state-of-emergency.html.

Chapter 3 Ideology, the Fall, and the Limits of Our Knowing

1. Karl Barth, *Romans* (London: Oxford University Press, 1953), 247.

2. Barth, *Romans*, 44.

3. Matthew Myer Boulton, *God against Religion: Rethinking Christian Theology through Worship* (Grand Rapids: Eerdmans, 2008), 76.

4. Boulton, *God against Religion*, 75.

5. Lewis Hyde, *Trickster Makes This World: Mischief, Myth, and Art* (New York: Farrar, Straus & Giroux, 1998), 36.

6. Stephen Mitchell, *The Book of Job* (San Francisco: North Point, 1987), 59.

7. Mitchell, *Book of Job*, 28.

8. Mitchell, *Book of Job*, 79.

9. Mitchell, *Book of Job*, 81.

10. Mitchell, *Book of Job*, 88.

11. Mitchell, *Book of Job*, 88.

12. Mitchell, *Book of Job*, 91.

13. Mitchell, *Book of Job*, 91.

14. Mitchell, *Book of Job*, 91.

15. Mitchell, *Book of Job*, xiv.

16. Mitchell, *Book of Job*, 64.

17. Susan Neiman, "The Rationality of the World: A Philosophical Reading of the Book of Job," Australian Broadcasting Corporation, updated January 20, 2021, https://www.abc.net.au/religion/philosophical-reading-of-the-book-of-job/11054038.

18. Russell Moore, *Losing Our Religion: An Altar Call for Evangelical America* (New York: Sentinel, 2023), 156.

Chapter 4 Authority, Violence, and the Erosion of Meaning

1. *Monty Python's Flying Circus*, series 2, episode 2, directed by Ian MacNaughton, written by Graham Chapman, John Cleese, Terry Gilliam, Eric Idle, Terry Jones, and Michael Palin, featuring Michael Palin as Cardinal Ximinez, *BBC*, September 22, 1970.

2. "John Paul II and the Galileo Affair," JP2 online, accessed May 31, 2024, https://jp2online.pl/en/publication/john-paul-ii-and-the-galileo-affair;UHVibGljYXRpb246MTE5.

3. Pss. 93:1; 104:5; 1 Chron. 16:30; Isa. 40:22.

4. Ps. 113:3; Matt. 5:45; 2 Sam. 23:4; Isa. 60:20; Rev. 21:23.

5. Galileo Galilei, "Letter to Madame Christina of Lorraine, Grand Duchess of Tuscany, 1615," accessed February 13, 2024, Interdisciplinary Encyclopedia of Religion & Science, https://inters.org/Galilei-Madame-Christina-Lorraine.

6. Michael J. Kruger, "What Is Spiritual Abuse?," Canon Fodder, February 8, 2021, https://www.michaeljkruger.com/what-is-spiritual-abuse.

7. Diane Langberg, "When the Sheep Are Preyed Upon," Ethics and Religious Liberty Commission, accessed February 13, 2024, https://erlc.com/resource-library/spotlight-articles/when-the-sheep-are-preyed-upon.

8. Hannah Arendt, *Between Past and Future: Eight Exercises in Political Thought* (New York: Penguin, 2006), 91.

9. Arendt, *Between Past and Future*, 92.

10. Arendt, *Between Past and Future*, chap. 3.

11. Arendt, *Between Past and Future*, 123.

12. Arendt, *Between Past and Future*, 124.

13. Arendt, *Between Past and Future*, 125.

14. Arendt, *Between Past and Future*, 126.

15. Arendt, *Between Past and Future*, 111.

16. Arendt, *Between Past and Future*, 132–33.

17. A concept introduced by Charles Taylor, "After Christendom," lecture, May 23, 2015, Thomas Merton Society, Bellarmine University, Louisville, Kentucky.

18. Charles Taylor calls this a "porous" self. Taylor, *A Secular Age* (Cambridge, MA: Belknap, 2007), 35.

19. Taylor, *Secular Age*, 3.

20. "What I'm interested in is how our sense of things, our cosmic imaginary, in other words, our whole background understanding and feel of the world has been transformed." Taylor, *Secular Age*, 325.

21. Taylor, *Secular Age*, 28.

22. Taylor, *Secular Age*, 541.

23. This idea is the central premise behind Jonah Goldberg's *Suicide of the West: How the Rebirth of Tribalism, Populism, Nationalism, and Identity Politics Is Destroying American Democracy* (New York: Crown Forum, 2018), in which Goldberg argues that liberal democracy and free markets are fundamentally against the grain of human nature and yet have brought about the greatest era of human flourishing in world history.

24. Taylor, *Secular Age*, 308, 309.

25. Taylor, *Secular Age*, 309.

26. Hannah Arendt, *The Origins of Totalitarianism* (New York: Meridian, 1958), 475.

27. "What prepares men for totalitarian domination in the non-totalitarian world is the fact that loneliness, once a borderline experience usually suffered in certain marginal social conditions like old age, has become an everyday experience of the ever-growing masses of our century." Arendt, *Origins of Totalitarianism*, 478.

28. Arendt consistently uses the world "isolation" here, but because I want to emphasize silence and solitude as a spiritual discipline later in the book, I'm preferring this word from the beginning. Just know when you read "solitude" or "isolation" (in her quotes), I intend them to mean the same thing.

29. Arendt, *Origins of Totalitarianism*, 475.

30. Goebbels, quoted in Arendt, *Origins of Totalitarianism*, 373n82.

31. Arendt, *Origins of Totalitarianism*, 477.

Chapter 5 Discovering the Banality of Evil

1. Doron Geller and Mitchell Bard, "The Capture of Nazi Criminal Adolf Eichmann—Operation Finale—and His Trial," Jewish Virtual Library, accessed February 7, 2024, https://www.jewishvirtuallibrary.org/the-capture-of-nazi-criminal-adolf-eichmann.

2. Hannah Arendt, letter to William Shawn, quoted in Elizabeth Young-Bruehl, *Hannah Arendt: For the Love of the World* (New Haven: Yale University Press, 1982), 329.

3. Hannah Arendt, *The Origins of Totalitarianism* (New York: Meridian, 1958), 459.

4. Arendt, *Origins of Totalitarianism*, 459.

5. Arendt, quoted in Amos Elon, introduction to Hannah Arendt, *Eichmann in Jerusalem: A Report on the Banality of Evil* (New York: Penguin, 2006), 14.

6. Arendt, *Eichmann in Jerusalem*, 351.

7. Geller and Bard, "Capture of Nazi Criminal Adolf Eichmann."

8. Arendt, *Eichmann in Jerusalem*, 351.

9. Arendt, *Eichmann in Jerusalem*, 352.

10. *The Dark Knight*, directed by Christopher Nolan, Warner Bros. Pictures, 2008.

11. Arendt, *Eichmann in Jerusalem*, 351.

12. Roger Berkowitz, "Did Eichmann Think?," *The American Interest*, September 7, 2014, http://www.the-american-interest.com/2014/09/07/did -eichmann-think.

13. Arendt, *Eichmann in Jerusalem*, 352.

14. Berkowitz, "Did Eichmann Think?"

15. Berkowitz, "Did Eichmann Think?"

16. Arendt, *Eichmann in Jerusalem*, 82, cited in Berkowitz, "Did Eichmann Think?"

17. Arendt, *Eichmann in Jerusalem*, 83.

18. Arendt, *Eichmann in Jerusalem*, 83.

19. Arendt, *Eichmann in Jerusalem*, 84.

20. Arendt, *Eichmann in Jerusalem*, 84–85.

21. Berkowitz, "Did Eichmann Think?"

22. Hannah Arendt, *The Life of the Mind: The Groundbreaking Investigation on How We Think* (New York: Harcourt Brace Jovanovich, 1981), 89.

23. Elon, introduction to Arendt, *Eichmann in Jerusalem*, 15.

24. Elon, introduction to Arendt, *Eichmann in Jerusalem*, 15.

25. Arendt, *Eichmann in Jerusalem*, 173.

26. The tone was softened somewhat in the versions of the articles that were collected and published in book form.

27. Kathleen B. Jones, "The Trial of Hannah Arendt," *Humanities* 35, no. 2 (March/April 2014), https://www.neh.gov/humanities/2014/marchapril /feature/the-trial-hannah-arendt.

28. Jones, "Trial of Hannah Arendt."

29. Hannah Arendt, "Personal Responsibility under Dictatorship," in Arendt, *Responsibility and Judgment* (New York: Schocken, 2003), 18. This reminds me too of someone who said of the 2016 election, "If you put a gun to my head and said you must vote for one of two people you find morally disqualified for the office, the ethical response is not to choose the lesser of two evils, but to simply say, 'Goodbye, cruel world.'" In other words, there is no such thing as being forced into immorality from an ethical standpoint; there is only the choice that Arendt highlights in this essay between "doing wrong" and "suffering wrong." Recent history suggests our capacity for suffering wrong is more fragile than we'd like to pretend.

30. D. T. Suzuki, *Zen and Japanese Culture* (New York: Pantheon, 1959), 114. This book was originally published in Japanese in 1938, when Suzuki's embrace of Japanese militaristic fascism was at its peak. It was translated into English in 1959, by which time Suzuki had long abandoned this posture.

31. Suzuki, *Zen and Japanese Culture*, 144.

32. Suzuki, *Zen and Japanese Culture*, 145.

Chapter 6 Eugene Peterson, Charlie Brown, and Resistance in Dark Times

1. Winn Collier, *A Burning in My Bones: The Authorized Biography of Eugene H. Peterson* (Colorado Springs: WaterBrook, 2021), 16.

2. Peterson, quoted in Collier, *Burning in My Bones*, 29.

3. Eugene Peterson, interview with Rodney Clapp, "Eugene Peterson: A Monk Out of Habit," *Christianity Today*, April 3, 1987, https://www.christianitytoday.com/ct/1987/april-3/eugene-peterson-monk-out-of-habit.html.

4. *A Charlie Brown Christmas*, directed by Bill Melendez, released December 9, 1965, produced by Lee Mendelson and Bill Melendez, distributed by United Feature Syndicate.

5. Aleksandr Solzhenitsyn, Nobel lecture, 1970, in *Nobel Lectures, Literature 1968–1980*, ed. Tore Frängsmyr (Singapore: World Scientific, 1993), available at https://www.nobelprize.org/prizes/literature/1970/solzhenitsyn/lecture.

Chapter 7 Solitude and Thinking

1. Hannah Arendt's Sonning Prize speech delivered on April 18, 1975, in Copenhagen is reprinted in full as the prologue to Hannah Arendt, *Responsibility and Judgment* (New York: Schocken, 2003), here 3.

2. Arendt, *Responsibility and Judgment*, 4.

3. Arendt, *Responsibility and Judgment*, 5.

4. Arendt, *Responsibility and Judgment*, 3.

5. Arendt, *Responsibility and Judgment*, 8.

6. Arendt, *Responsibility and Judgment*, 11.

7. One could make the case (and many have) that these classical distinctions are overly simple, particularly when you examine a society that takes religion seriously. One could also criticize Arendt (and many have) for being overly celebratory of a culture that was exclusive of minorities and women. Arendt might actually agree with such critiques, but there is some value to be found in using these categories as helpful, if imperfect, shorthand—especially once we begin to look at the impact of the social, below.

8. Charles Taylor, *A Secular Age* (Cambridge, MA: Belknap, 2007), 481.

9. Hannah Arendt, *The Origins of Totalitarianism* (New York: Meridian, 1958), 52.

10. Arendt, *Responsibility and Judgment*, 11.

11. Arendt, *Responsibility and Judgment*, 12.

12. Arendt, *Responsibility and Judgment*, 13.

13. Arendt, *Responsibility and Judgment*, 13–14.

14. Augustine, *Confessions* 1.1.

15. Hannah Arendt, *The Human Condition*, 2nd ed. (Chicago: University of Chicago Press, 2018), 76.

16. David Foster Wallace, *The Pale King* (New York: Little, Brown), 87.

17. Beth Moore, *All My Knotted-Up Life: A Memoir* (Carol Stream, IL: Tyndale, 2023), 240.

18. Moore, *All My Knotted-Up Life*, 241.

19. Moore, *All My Knotted-Up Life*, 245.

Chapter 8 Storytelling and Culture Making

1. Keith Richards, with James Fox, *Life* (New York: Little, Brown, 2010), 462.

2. "Cody Rhodes and Paul Heyman Get Personal | WWE Raw Highlights 2/6/23 | WWE on USA," YouTube video, 9:34, posted by WWE on USA, February 6, 2023, https://youtu.be/EGDXvkriDZE.

3. "Best WWE Interview of 2017—The Undertaker 'Out of Character' w/ Ed Young," YouTube video, 37:38, posted by Ed Young, September 30, 2018, https://youtu.be/4mcd8BAjU0c.

4. *Julius Caesar* by William Shakespeare, act 3, scene 2.

5. A "heel" is a wrestler who performs the role of the unsympathetic antagonist or adversary in a staged wrestling match.

6. Hannah Arendt, *The Human Condition*, 2nd ed. (Chicago: University of Chicago Press, 2018), 176–77.

7. Arendt, *Human Condition*, 177.

8. Aleksandr Solzhenitsyn, Nobel lecture, 1970, in *Nobel Lectures, Literature 1968–1980*, ed. Tore Frängsmyr (Singapore: World Scientific, 1993), available at https://www.nobelprize.org/prizes/literature/1970/solzhenitsyn/lecture.

9. Solzhenitsyn, Nobel lecture.

10. Solzhenitsyn, Nobel lecture.

Chapter 9 Worship, or Light in Dark Times

1. Greg L. Hawkins and Cally Parkinson, *Reveal* (South Barrington, IL: Willow Creek Association, 2007), 51.

2. Hannah Arendt, *Thinking without a Banister: Essays in Understanding, 1953–1975* (New York: Schocken, 2018), 144.

3. Augustine, *Confessions* 1.1.

4. Technically, Calvin called it a "forge of idols" in the *Institutes* 1.11.45, but I like this rendering.

5. David Foster Wallace, commencement speech, Kenyon College, Gambier, Ohio, May 21, 2005, available at http://bulletin-archive.kenyon.edu/x4280.html.

6. The image of the poet and rationalist comes from G. K. Chesterton, *Orthodoxy* (Mumbai: Sanage, 2023), 17.

Afterword

1. Robert Nicholson, "A New Year's Resolution, An Ancient Evil: Combatting Antisemitism in 2019," *Providence*, January 1, 2019, https://providence mag.com/2019/01/a-new-years-resolution-an-ancient-evil-the-fight-against -antisemitism-in-2019.

MIKE COSPER has been creating music, radio shows, and podcasts for more than twenty years. He produced and hosted *The Rise and Fall of Mars Hill* podcast and is director of podcasts at *Christianity Today*. He also cohosts a weekly podcast called *The Bulletin*, leads cohorts for church leaders, and is the author of six books, including *Recapturing the Wonder*. He and his family live in Louisville, Kentucky.

Connect with Mike:

mikecosper.net

 mikecosper    @mikedcosper   @mikecosper